DØ169569

701 SENTENCE SERMONS

Attention-Getting Quotes for
Church Signs, Bulletins,
Newsletters, and Sermons

L. James Harvey

Kregel
Publications

701 Sentence Sermons: Attention-Getting Quotes for Church Signs, Bulletins, Newsletters, and Sermons

© 2000 by L. James Harvey

Published by Kregel Publications, a division of Kregel, Inc., P.O. Box 2607, Grand Rapids, MI 49501. Kregel Publications provides trusted, biblical publications for Christian growth and service. Your comments and suggestions are valued.

Cover design © 2000 by Kregel Publications

Library of Congress Cataloging-in-Publication Data
Harvey, L. James.
 701 sentence sermons: attention-getting quotes for church signs, bulletins, newsletters, and sermons / by L. James Harvey.
  Includes index.
  p. cm.
 1. Church signs. 2. Advertising—Churches. I. Title. II. Title: Seven hundred one sentence sermons. III. Title: Seven hundred and one sentence sermons.
BV653.7.H37 1999 254'.3—dc21 99-33804
                  CIP

ISBN 978-0-8254-2889-0

Printed in the United States of America

5 6 7 8 9 / 11 10 09 08 07

Contents

Acknowledgments / 4

Introduction   The Bouquet / 5

Part One

Chapter 1   Sentence Sermons / 9
Chapter 2   The Purpose of Sentence Sermons / 12
Chapter 3   Church Signs / 15
Chapter 4   Sign Policies / 18
Chapter 5   Sign Strategies / 23
Chapter 6   Other Uses for Sentence Sermons / 25
Chapter 7   Sentence Sermon Resources / 27
Chapter 8   Sentence Sermons in Sermons / 32
Chapter 9   How to Use This Book / 34

Part Two

Chapter 10   701 Ideas for Sentence Sermons / 39
Index   Sentence Sermon Topics and Sources / 155

Acknowledgments

Many people have made contributions in one way or another to this publication. Some gave encouragement, some contributed sentence sermons, and some provided ideas. I would like to say a special thanks to the following for playing a part in developing the sign ministry at St. Paul's Church and for providing material for this book.

Butch and Ann Aurich

Ina Bolton

Bill and Arbeleta Burdette

Alfred and Naomi Cain

Paul and Hildy Cardaci

Pat Jones

John and Martha Lane

Charles and Ruth Long

Robert Loving

Charles and Yvonne Maddox

Marty Martin

Phillip Massay

Judy and Shawn McClosky

Steve and Kathie Nicholas

Gordon Sommers

Donn and Delores Stansbury

Elsie Taylor

Jack and Mona Voden

Last but not least, thanks goes to my loving wife of forty-eight years, Jackie, for her encouragement, skillful editing, and advice.

The Bouquet

It was a hot morning. The red alert for air quality had been announced, and it wasn't even nine o'clock. I decided to go early to change the church sign for the next week, before the heat became even more suffocating.

As I drove to the church, I was thinking about the events of the last two days that had been precipitated by the death of John Kennedy Jr., his wife, and his sister-in-law, in a plane crash. I decided to look for a sentence sermon for that week that would say something to passersby about the Christian view of death.

The sign I was about to take down was related to the horrible killings at Columbine High School in Colorado. It repeated the words of Cassie Bernall, the heroic young woman who, when asked by one of the killers, "Do you believe in God?" said, "Yes, I believe in God!" She was shot dead instantly. Cassie had been a beautiful young woman—recently converted to Christ after years of self-indulgence and drugs—and now her life was snuffed out. Her testimony was being spread across America, and Christian young people were repeating her words everywhere, "Yes, I believe in God!"

I had decided to put up a sentence sermon that said, "DEATH TO THE CHRISTIAN IS A TRANSFER TO THE HOME OFFICE." I hoped it would remind people passing by that Christians view this life as just a temporary assignment, and that one day we will all be assigned permanently to "headquarters," where we will be in the eternal presence of our heavenly Father.

After selecting the letters for the sentence sermon, I walked the fifty or so yards from the church to the sign, which sits at a major intersection in front of the church. I took out the key and opened the sliding panel that allows access to the letters. As I turned the key, I became aware of an object lying at the base of the sign. When I looked down, I saw a small bouquet of flowers. They were simple flowers from a garden, carefully wrapped in a pink sheet of paper. My guess is that some young person had placed the bouquet there as an unspoken tribute to Cassie.

Cassie is now at corporate headquarters, but her testimony and her words live on to inspire young Christians around the world. How marvelous it is that our God can take an evil act and turn it into something so positive. In death, Cassie Bernall is influencing young Christians in a way she might never have been able to, had she lived. She certainly had a profound effect on one young person who took some time to lay a small, yet meaningful, tribute before our church sign.

And what of the church sign? It had provided a way for a mourning congregation to express solidarity with the victims of the Columbine massacre and to proclaim anew the message Cassie died to give. It had also served as a focal point for a simple expression of gratitude. The church sign had served God well.

While its role is not always as obvious as this, examples of the effectiveness of a church sign are manifold. It is my sincere hope and prayer that this book will enhance your own church sign ministry.

Part One

CHAPTER 1

Sentence Sermons

A man enters a church with tears in his eyes. He gives the church staff twenty dollars and says the church sign that day was just what he has needed. The church staff has never seen him before.

A woman stops in a church office and says her husband's corporation, headquartered in another state, wants to use the message on the church sign in their newsletter. She wants to know who said it, in order to give credit.

A Baptist church reports that over several years it has averaged better than one new visiting family a month because of what they saw on the church sign.

A man stops by while a church member is changing the church sign. He says he is a local radio announcer, and he has been using the words on the sign in his radio broadcasts. He says his station manager loves them and wants to know where the church gets its messages.

A man writes a letter to a church thanking the congregation for saving his life. He drove by the church one day intent on committing suicide because everything had collapsed around him. He saw a message on the church sign that changed his mind.

These illustrations are all true. They happened because some churches have put up signs with meaningful messages on them. I like to call those messages sentence sermons, because that's what they are.

These sentence sermons, some from Scripture, some from contemporary thought, and some from sages of the past, carry in their limited wording a truth about life. They, in effect, encapsulate a sermon in a sentence and give people a thought that is profound, easy to remember, and often humorous.

Businesses for centuries have used catchy phrases, humorous statements, and attractive ads to sell their wares and present information about their products. Christians have been more timid about using these devices in reaching out to the unchurched, perhaps for fear of being seen as a business or of being too glitzy. Churches have been, by and large, conservative and staid organizations. The only neon signs used consistently in the past have been the "Jesus Saves" signs on storefront missions in the poor section of town. Any other church signs have been used only to tell people when services are, and what the sermon topic is for the next Sunday.

This is beginning to change, and a marvelous new opportunity is spreading across the country. Churches are setting up signs in front of their buildings, and they are using them to present Christian truth. These churches are displaying sentence sermons in sound bites for the drivers who pass the building each day. New sermons are put up periodically, usually weekly or twice a week, and the results are amazing.

People are finding Christ, joining the church, changing their lives, and getting daily truth injections, all through a very inexpensive yet effective device—the church sign.

In the information age, we now have facts coming at us faster and faster, often in the form of bites or small packages of data. TV producers change the picture frequently lest they lose our attention. We want things to be quick, packaged, and interesting. The church should recognize this reality and work to present God's truth in a modern and catchy fashion. A church sign ministry is one way to do this. It can be effective without watering down the truth or compromising the more traditional church programs.

Every church that has used this method of outreach for any length of time has stories to tell like those above. This book has been written to encourage you to develop a sentence sermon ministry and to show you how best to do it.

CHAPTER 2

The Purpose of Sentence Sermons

Throughout history, people have sought to encapsulate and convey truths in short sentences or phrases that can be easily remembered. We call these brief statements aphorisms, proverbs, adages, maxims, or slogans. Who hasn't heard or said the following?

1. A stitch in time saves nine.
2. The grass is always greener on the other side of the fence.
3. The proof is in the pudding.
4. The Devil is in the details.
5. Beauty is only skin-deep.
6. The early bird gets the worm.
7. Birds of a feather flock together.
8. A bird in the hand is worth two in the bush.
9. Two wrongs don't make a right.
10. Strike while the iron is hot.

These sayings remind us of truths that are far more profound than the few simple words that compose them. When we use them in a conversation, we convey a major truth or concept in "shorthand." The person listening is immediately aware of a principle or logical construct that needs no further explanation.

In short, throughout history we have sought to package concepts and ideas so that we can communicate them quickly and efficiently.

Christians should recognize the value of this process and do whatever they can to present the truth of God in easily understood phrases. One of the best places to do this is in front of or near a church on a sign that is clearly visible to passersby twenty-four hours a day. There is no limit to the good such a sign can do and to the ways God will use our messages in the lives of those passing by. As Christians we believe God, through his Holy Spirit, is at work in the world. When we pick out and display sentence sermons, the Holy Spirit will use them in magnificent ways, ways that we cannot begin to anticipate or understand.

The Sunday sermon is essential, and nothing here is intended in any way to minimize its importance. But the sermon is usually a once-a-Sunday event delivered to people who are already members of the church, along with perhaps a few visitors. Since the average church is around two hundred members, that means around one hundred and fifty people will hear a sermon on any given Sunday. In addition, studies show that people remember very little out of a Sunday sermon, even right after it is heard. After a few days, practically nothing is retained. Of course, this does not mean sermons are unimportant, particularly for the instruction and spiritual growth of the faithful. As a friend once said, "A sermon is like a meal. I can't remember every meal I have ever had, but I know each one did me some good." However, a nugget of truth delivered or remembered at the precise moment it is needed can have a tremendous effect, on church members and non-church members alike. This is where the sentence sermon comes into its own.

A church sign might be passed each day by hundreds or even thousands of vehicles. Christians have the opportunity to reach out and affect the lives of these passing people, many of whom have never darkened the door of a church. We also have the opportunity to demonstrate to them what we believe. Many people visit churches because of what they have read on signs outside. Some could not have been reached in any other way. Can we afford to pass up a chance like this?

Christians must look at every available means for delivering the truth of God to those who need it. Sentence sermons are not intended to compete with or replace sermons, Bible studies, church publications, or any of the other ways we have of communicating our message. Instead they are an effective, inexpensive addition to our traditional methods of outreach.

Times are changing. In the past the sign in front of a church was only used to give passersby the name of the church, the times of worship, and the name of the pastor. A sign like this was designed to be read by people who were on foot, and it typically used one-inch letters. Now cars speed by our churches, and correspondingly the technology of signs has changed. From one-sided, black and white, horizontally-placed boards, we now have moved on to two-sided, beautifully colored, perpendicular signs with six- to eight-inch letters. These signs can even be back-lit for twenty-four-hour use. Countless drivers pass by and read them daily. Churches have a wonderful opportunity. Don't miss it!

CHAPTER 3

Church Signs

Church signs have evolved over the years. New technology has made them more attractive and much easier to use. From the old dull boards placed parallel to the street we now have graduated to today's well-lit, attractive signs, situated perpendicular to the roadway, and carrying catchy sentence sermons as well as other basic church information. Some larger churches even have computerized signs with programmed messages.

Attractive, functional signs can be purchased and erected for as little as two thousand to three thousand dollars. They can also cost as much as eighteen thousand dollars to forty-five thousand if they have an electronic message center with changing messages. The majority of churches will spend between four thousand to five thousand dollars, which will buy a beautiful, customized, internally-lit sign.

When purchasing a church sign, you should consider the following recommendations.

1. Make sure your sign is enclosed and secure. This will prevent vandals, weather, and pranksters from causing problems.
2. Make sure there is a strong contrast between the letters and the sign background. A white background with black letters is recommended, though an ivory background with brown letters

can also be effective. Currently, fewer than 25 percent of the signs are ivory while 75 percent or more are black and white. Remember, the purpose is to make the sign as readable as possible for drivers passing the church.

3. The sign should be perpendicular to the road so both sides can be read by drivers. It should also be as close to the road as zoning regulations permit for quicker, easier sight lines (see number 7 below).

4. The sign should be lit, preferably from the inside, for twenty-four-hour use. The sign lights can be put on a timer or attached to a photoelectric switch that will turn the sign on and off based on the light available or the time of day.

5. Letters should be clean and crisp. Avoid using script or decorative letters, as they make reading the sign more difficult. It is recommended that you use a sans serif typeface, the familiar block letters, and that you use all capitals. It is better to use bold rather than slimmer letters. Numbers could be ordered in a different color to add contrast. Red is popular for this purpose. Again, everything should be done for easy readability from the roadway.

6. Before buying a sign, test to see what size and type of letters are best. Do an experiment with a poster and drive by at the average speed cars go by your church. Research estimates that the average time a driver has to read a sign is five seconds. You may wish to pass by signs at other churches to make sure the type and size of letters you order are the best for your situation. The company you select should be willing to help you design the best possible sign for motorists. Letters at least six to eight inches in height are usually recommended. A sign company executive, with many years of experience in the business, says the rule of thumb is "the bigger the better." He also says that he has never had customers complain about getting letters that were too big, but some have been sorry they didn't get bigger ones. Remember, the idea is to make the messages easily read in about five seconds. Big, under these conditions, is better.

7. Put your sign as close to the road as you are allowed. Many

areas have zoning laws covering size and placement of signs. Be sure you are in compliance with the law. The city hall or county courthouse is usually the best place to start checking out regulations.

8. Make the sign as attractive as possible. The name of the church, its denomination, its logo, and other permanent information can be placed in eye-catching colors at the top of, or surrounding, the message box.

9. Be sure you order enough letters so you do not find yourself in the frustrating position of having a dynamite sentence sermon but not enough letters to put it up. The sign company can give you advice on this issue, but err on the side of ordering too many letters rather than too few.

10. The sign should be at least four by six feet and have no more than five lines of type. Four is the most common number, although three or five are often used.

You have studied the situation and have selected and installed the best sign for your church. Now you must decide how the sign is to be used and who will control it!

CHAPTER 4

Sign Policies

One thing is for certain, once the sign is up people will start asking to have things posted on it. Some will want their programs publicized, while others will want to have anniversaries or graduations recognized. Some will want only scriptural verses, while still others will want words of wisdom from famous people. Some may even want statements posted on it that have social or political overtones.

One church put a message on their sign opposing drug use. Unfortunately, this led to vandalism. Their sign was not enclosed, and a great deal of damage was done. Another church, one that has had a sign ministry for a number of years and has routinely received positive comments on it, had a serious complaint lodged over a message seen as critical of welfare recipients.

Does this mean a church should avoid messages that deal with social issues? Not at all. But it does mean that care must be taken. Along with the great good it can do, a church sign has the potential for causing problems. It must, therefore, be controlled by a set of policies.

A church must decide what the primary purpose of the sign is and how it is to be used. Is it to reach the unchurched, or is it to speak to members and those who already know the Lord? Will only Scripture verses be posted, and if so, which version of the Bible will they be taken from? If words other than Scripture are used, who will select them, and what sources are appropriate for finding them? Will special church events be publicized, or will the sign be used solely for sentence sermons? If the sign has two sides, will they both say the same thing or different things? Who will change the message and when?

Unless these and other issues are dealt with ahead of time, conflicts will arise. A formal sign policy should be drawn up and approved by the church governing board in order to avoid problems.

The following is a sample of a possible sign policy statement.

Sample Church Sign Policy Statement

Our church sign presents a significant opportunity for ministry. It is essential that we have policies and procedures in place to maximize effective use of the sign while avoiding conflicts.

Vision Statement

The church sign will be used to further the church's mission to the community by presenting Christian truths through sentence sermons, by announcing special events, and by serving as a communication bridge.

Policies Regarding Church Sign

1. The joint board will annually appoint a sign master upon recommendation of the pastor.
2. The sign master will have the responsibility of changing the sign as needed and of selecting the sentence sermon for the week.
3. The sign master, the pastor, and a third person, selected from the evangelism committee upon recommendation of the pastor and approved by the church board, will form the sign committee.
4. The sign master will be responsible for developing and maintaining a list of messages that must be preapproved by the sign committee for use. This list should provide a reserve of no less than three month's worth of sign messages at all times.

5. The sign committee will be responsible for preapproving all signs and for establishing policies governing the placement of signs within the following guidelines:

   A. The primary purpose of the sign is to reach out to the community with Christian truth.

   B. The sign may be used to announce special programs at the church that are of interest to the general community. This use of the sign will be limited so as not to disrupt the continuity of the sentence sermon ministry or in any way reduce interest in the sign. Announcements of church events may be placed on the sign only by a vote of two-thirds of the sign committee or by church board decision. As a rule, this will not be done two weeks in a row and will not exceed seven to eight times per year.

   C. The sign will be changed weekly or more often, with no sign remaining up longer than a week unless unanimously agreed to by the sign committee or by church board request.

   D. The sign will not be used to congratulate people, to announce birthdays, anniversaries, or graduations without the unanimous approval of the sign committee or by approval of the church board.

The preceding policy covers the necessary issues and provides a framework within which issues can be resolved.

Who will actually be responsible for changing the sign? It is best to have one person in charge. This way, the responsibility is fixed, and a regular pattern will be more easily established. A church staff member or any member of the church who feels a special call to this type of ministry could be selected. Someone who is retired would be ideal. It is a good idea to give such a person a title, to recognize the importance of the position. Sign master, sign captain, or sign manager are some of the names that might be considered.

The sign should be considered part of the church's ministry. After all, the church is presenting truth to the community through it so in a very real way the sign is speaking for the church. Since this is a form of outreach, with significant implications for evangelism, any outreach or evangelism committees of the church should be represented on the sign committee.

It is imperative that the selection of what goes on the sign should not be left to one person. In the policy above, the task is left to a committee that always includes the pastor. This allows for a screening of material and input from various perspectives. At the same time, the committee should be kept small enough that decisions can be made quickly since current events can sometimes dictate a sudden change in message. For example, when Mother Teresa died recently it was near the end of the week. By the next Monday one of her quotes was up on a church's sign. This was far more effective than if it had appeared a week or so later.

The usual policy is for a sign committee to develop a list of preapproved messages that the sign master can post without further consultation. With a small committee, however, any new message could be approved quickly over the phone if necessary. Since there is always the potential for controversy, it is best to have more than one person deciding what should be presented in the name of the church.

It is important to change the sign regularly on the same day of the week so the community will come to expect and look forward to the new message. People will soon get into the habit of looking for it as they go by. Sunday evening or Monday morning seems to be the most logical times to change it, if this is to be done weekly. If the sign is to be changed twice a week, Sunday/Monday and Wednesday/Thursday would seem logical. The actual days and times matter little. The important thing is that it is done consistently.

The most typical period for leaving a message on the sign is one week, though many churches will change it twice a week. Twice a week is possible, but every day is too difficult. Besides, having a sign up for three to seven days allows motorists to pass it several times. This repetition gives them time to think about what they have read and possibly to memorize it as well.

Lastly, it is important to have a clear mission statement in place so that those directly involved, as well as all church members, have a full and mutual understanding of what can and cannot appear on the sign. This will prevent any problems and unpleasantness down the road.

CHAPTER 5

Sign Strategies

The sign can be used for different strategies. It can be aimed at attracting new members, for example. In this case, the messages might be humorous and catchy, with quotes from prominent people. If the sign is meant to fortify Christians and church members in their faith, the messages might be drawn from Scripture and deal more particularly with spiritual matters.

Anyone involved in a church sign ministry should expect some tension to develop between those who want all Scripture on the one hand, and those who want a broader source for the sentence sermons on the other. Churches with a two-sided sign might use one side of the sign for scriptural texts and the other side for popular sayings. It is also possible to rotate different types of sayings from week to week. Note that of the 701 sentence sermons included in chapter 10 of this book, the first 546 are more secular and the rest are scriptural. Those wishing to separate them can easily do so.

The church sign has tremendous potential as an inexpensive yet powerful outreach tool. It is a proven method for bringing visitors to the church. From a purely economic perspective, new members generated by the effective use of the sign will pay for it many times over with their tithes and offerings. Any opposition to a new sign based on cost can easily be countered by statistical data showing the number of new members likely to be attracted by it and by their predicted contributions to the church. The church sign is a wise investment both financially and, more importantly, eternally, as through it the Great Commission of Jesus Christ is carried out.

Pray each time a message is put up. Pray that it will touch the souls of those who pass by. Good results will occur. There are churches and organizations all over the country that can attest to this fact.

Go out armed with the truth and start a "sound bite ministry."

CHAPTER 6

Other Uses for Sentence Sermons

The sentence sermons presented here can be used in a variety of ways to reach people with the truth. Here are some suggestions for starting your own "sound bite ministry."

1. Newsletters: If your company has a newsletter, perhaps a sentence sermon could be included in each issue. If the company is a large public one, it may not be possible to include scriptural messages, but there should be no resistance to those sentence sermons that present general wisdom. A church newsletter could include one or more sentence sermons in every issue.
2. Letters: Whenever you write a letter, you might wish to include a sound bite of wisdom for the recipient to consider.
3. Checks: Some banks allow you to print brief sayings on your checks, which can be read by anyone who handles them. You might choose a sentence sermon for one set of checks and change it on the next set.
4. E-Mail: It is easy to include brief sentence sermons in the e-mail messages you send to friends and business associates. This would set your correspondence apart from the rest, making your messages stand out.

5. Web Pages: If you have a web page, it would be easy to include a message every day or week. A "thought for the day" would add interest whether your web page is purely personal or business related.
6. Bulletin Boards: If your employer has a bulletin board, you might ask whether you could pin up a weekly sound bite. Few employers would object to a short message for everyone to consider, and perhaps you could even put up a biblical quotation on occasion.
7. Blackboards: In educational environments, teachers can easily write on a small part of a blackboard a truth that students might see and consider.
8. Business Signs: If you own a business, you may wish to use the message center for sound bites of wisdom. The business name, logo, operating hours, and so forth, could go on the sign in permanent lettering, but the message center itself could be used for a sentence sermon. This would make the sign a focal point of community interest, allow the business to establish its character and integrity, and provide a community service.

Many years ago, when cars went more slowly and there were no super-highways, the Burma Shave Company had billboards along the roads of America that displayed witty bits of wisdom. As you drove along, you would see a series of signs, each with a few words on it, leading to the final "punch line" and the inevitable advertisement for Burma Shave. People looked for these signs as they traveled and often shared the sayings with friends. Older people still remember them with a smile. The point is that giving people a smile and bit of truth creates a good feeling about a company and its products. It is an excellent advertising tool. If a company does not wish to cross into religion and Scripture with its messages, it could simply use the sayings in the first part of chapter 10 of this book.

The places these bits of truth can be used are almost unlimited. Think of the endeavor as scattering seeds, like the biblical parable of the sower. Some seeds will fall on fertile soil, and they will make a good crop. If we faithfully scatter, we can be certain God will use our efforts to bring forth the fruit.

CHAPTER 7

Sentence Sermon Resources

Where can good sentence sermons be found? This is a logical question for anyone embarking on a "sound bite ministry." Fortunately, there are many sources. Sentence sermons can be found almost anywhere.

To begin with, there are 701 of them in Part Two of this book. Moreover, the Bible is a treasure trove. The book of Proverbs has more wisdom for living packed into its pages than any other book ever written. Many helpful verses are included here, but many more will be found on the pages of Scripture. The Psalms also include a wealth of material. And another wonderful source can be found in the Gospels, in the words of Jesus. Using a Bible with Christ's words printed in red makes them easier to spot.

Most bookstores have books of quotations and meditations that could provide a valuable collection of sayings. Many ministries and denominations also publish books or monthly booklets of daily devotions. These books usually have a Scripture verse for the day and often a saying or statement that summarizes the content presented. This material can be modified to fit a sign or the space available for a sentence sermon.

Some good resources of this kind are:

> *Our Daily Bread:* A daily devotional published quarterly by the Radio Bible Class (RBC Ministries), Grand Rapids,

Michigan 49555-0001. This can be ordered directly or through their web site: http://www.rbc.net/.

In Touch: A daily devotional published monthly by In Touch Ministries, P.O. Box 7900, Atlanta, Georgia 30357. This daily devotional can be read on the internet at: http://www.intouch.org. If you wish to e-mail them they can be reached at: magazine@intouch.org.

Moravian Daily Texts: An annual booklet of daily devotions available through the Moravian Church either at 1021 Center Street, Bethlehem, Pennsylvania 18018 or 500 South Church Street, Winston-Salem, North Carolina 27101.

When you use the above material, or any other material, you will often find that adjustments need to be made to make the messages fit comfortably onto a church sign. For example, the typical sign may have four lines, each with about twenty spaces for letters. That means that many longer Scripture verses and messages will not fit. In any case, you will want to keep all messages as short as possible in order to make them readable from cars passing the church.

Fortunately, adjustments are easy. In some cases, messages of Scripture can be presented without placing the whole verse on the sign. In other cases, certain words might be left out without changing the meaning of the material. You may wish to leave attributions or scriptural references out altogether to give more room. Here is an example from a quotation found on the internet. The original quotation was as follows:

I am persuaded that love and humility are the highest attainments in the School of Christ and the brightest evidences that He is indeed our master.

—John Newton (1725–1807)

As is, the passage could not fit on a church sign, and even if it could, it is too long to be read by drivers. Yet the essentials could easily be put on a sign. The result might look like this:

LOVE AND HUMILITY
ARE THE HIGHEST
ATTAINMENTS IN THE
SCHOOL OF CHRIST

On a normal four-line sign, there would be no room for an attribution to John Newton, but the church office could have the information on hand should anyone ask for it. This method of condensing material allows for truths to be put on the sign that would otherwise be excluded for lack of space.

Normally, attributions and scriptural references are placed on the bottom line to the right so they would be the last thing read. For nonscriptural messages, it is recommended that attributions not be used at all unless they add some significance to the message. As in the earlier example, attributing a sentence sermon to Mother Teresa the week after she died was critical because people were grieving her death, and it made the message so much more moving. On the other hand, attributing a message composed by an obscure sixteenth-century French poet, whom no one knows anyway, only takes up space on the sign and adds little to the significance of the material.

The sentence sermons that follow in this book have been designed for a typical church sign, one that has four lines of type and twenty spaces for letters per line. You may find that the size of your letters differs from those we used. You may also find that some letters (e.g., *W*'s and *M*'s) take up more space than others (e.g., *I*'s and *L*'s). Normally, each line should be centered. The best thing to do is set up the sign as best as you can and then step back and test it for balance and readability. The final test is, of course, to drive by yourself to be sure it looks right and can be easily read.

You may wish to modify or change the sentence sermons that follow, based on your sign, its location, and its mission. For example, one of the messages is:

LOVE HELD CHRIST
ON THE CROSS
NOT NAILS

That message is only eight words long and can easily be read at just about any speed. However, if your church is fortunate enough to be located by a stop sign or traffic light, where ease of reading is greater, you might want to lengthen the message a little and post it as follows:

NAILS DID NOT HOLD
CHRIST TO THE CROSS
IT WAS LOVE
FOR YOU AND ME

This version is basically the same but with a more personal touch. Use your best judgment based on the variables and opportunities presented by your sign.

When messages are posted, phrasing, punctuation, and line breaks should all be considered and used to help the reading and presentation of thought. For example, a message could be as follows:

KNOW THE TRUTH AND
THE TRUTH WILL MAKE
YOU FREE
—JOHN 8:32

However, it would be more meaningful if the three phrases were each on a separate line as follows:

KNOW THE TRUTH
AND THE TRUTH
WILL MAKE YOU FREE
—JOHN 8:32

You may not always be able to put separate thoughts or phrases on single lines, but when you can it helps the reader grasp the truth presented more easily.

Punctuation marks like apostrophes, commas, dashes, periods, ampersands, and so forth, can be used as appropriate to shorten messages and to break phrases for better understanding. Quotation marks are not necessary because all the messages are assumed to be quotations, and the marks simply take up space. However, on occasion they should be used for emphasis, as in this case:

NEWS BULLETIN FROM GOD TO RACISTS: "HEAVEN IS INTEGRATED"

One last point needs to be made. Since the sign represents your church or organization, and you want to project an image of competence, always be absolutely certain your spelling and grammar are correct. Check and double-check to insure that the sign message is absolutely right in every aspect.

CHAPTER 8

Sentence Sermons
in Sermons

Sentence sermons can be used effectively to enhance the understanding and retention of material presented in the traditional Sunday sermon. As mentioned earlier, research shows that the average churchgoer does not remember much from a Sunday sermon. Memory can be enhanced, however, if the pastor uses a sentence sermon to focus attention on the particular truth he is presenting. Here are a couple of ways this can be done.

1. In congregations with a formal Sunday worship style, the pastor could develop a sentence sermon as he prepares his sermon. This brief, one-sentence statement would encapsulate the basic truth of the message. It could then be included in the Sunday bulletin, mentioned during and after the sermon for emphasis, and placed on one side of the church sign so parishioners would be reminded of it during the week. The following Sunday, the pastor could challenge the members to remember the sentence sermon from the previous Sunday. This repetition and reinforcement could greatly improve the congregation's retention of the basic Sunday message and increase its impact on their lives.

2. For churches with an open worship style, where interaction between the pastor and congregation is encouraged, another approach could be used. The pastor could challenge the congregation before each service to listen carefully and, following the sermon, jointly determine what sentence sermon might sum up the message. The pastor might well be surprised at the suggestions, but the process would provide great feedback on the sermon. The sentence sermon chosen could then be used in the bulletin, on the church sign, and it could be mentioned the next Sunday to further reinforce the message.

We know that people learn and retain material through repetition and by linking it to knowledge they already have. The sentence sermon approach has the potential of helping pastors and congregations remember the truths of God more effectively.

CHAPTER 9

How to Use This Book

Because people's interests, needs, and interpretations may differ, a variety of sentence sermons have been presented in the pages that follow. Some are humorous, some are straightforward, and still others are designed to make people think. Some come from Scripture, some from Christian thinkers, and others from secular sources that present basic truths. People will react differently to the same sentence sermon depending on their perceptions and theological perspectives. Careful selection is essential to avoid controversy.

Churches will differ in their choice of sentence sermons depending on their location, the character of the majority of people who pass the church (e.g., their educational level, socioeconomic background, religious affiliation or lack of it), and the primary purpose of their sign.

If you are part of a church committee charged with the responsibility of a church sign, you can use the following rating system to select sermons that will be the best for your individual circumstances. Committee members can each take a book and rate every sentence sermon on the five-point rating scale presented here, circling the number that best indicates how they feel about it. For example, if they think the sermon is outstanding and should have priority, they can circle the 5. If it is very good, but there are better ones that should be used first, they can circle the 4. Those of less merit can be rated 3 and 2, with the understanding that they will be used after all the 4s and 5s. The 1 should be reserved for those not wanted at all. It is the veto rating.

The recommended scale is as follows:

1	2	3	4	5
(Poor)	(Weak)	(Average)	(Very Good)	(Best)
Do not use	Use others first	Use 4s & 5s first	Use 5s first	Use first

After each committee member has rated all of the sentence sermons, one of the members can average out the results, producing a list your committee feels is best for your situation. The high-priority messages can then be given to your sign master.

If you are an individual using the sentence sermons in one of the many other ways mentioned earlier, you can use the same rating system for yourself. This will help you readily identify those messages you most want to use and allow you to locate them easily and quickly.

Read, enjoy, and use the sentence sermons that follow!

Part Two

CHAPTER 10

701 Ideas for Sentence Sermons

1.

**GIVE ALL YOU CAN
BECAUSE NO ONE EVER
SAW A HEARSE PULLING
A U-HAUL**

Rating: 1 2 3 4 5 Date Used:

2.

**GOD IS DEAD
—NIETZSCHE
NIETZSCHE IS DEAD!
—GOD**

Rating: 1 2 3 4 5 Date Used:

3.

**TO LEAD THE
ORCHESTRA ONE MUST
TURN ONE'S BACK
ON THE CROWD**

Rating: 1 2 3 4 5 Date Used:

4.

TROUBLES LIKE BABIES GROW LARGER THROUGH NURSING

Rating: 1 2 3 4 5   Date Used:

5.

GOD BRINGS PEOPLE INTO DEEP WATER NOT TO DROWN THEM BUT TO CLEANSE THEM

Rating: 1 2 3 4 5   Date Used:

6.

TO CONFESS A FAULT FREELY IS THE NEXT BEST THING TO BEING FREE OF IT

Rating: 1 2 3 4 5   Date Used:

7.

THERE IS NO RIGHT WAY TO DO THE WRONG THING

Rating: 1 2 3 4 5   Date Used:

8.

NO ONE EVER CHOKED TO DEATH SWALLOWING THEIR OWN PRIDE

Rating: 1 2 3 4 5   Date Used:

9.

CHILDREN HAVE MORE NEED OF MODELS THAN CRITICS

Rating: 1 2 3 4 5   Date Used:

10.

FAITH IS THE CONTINUATION OF REASON

Rating: 1   2   3   4   5   Date Used:

11.

ALL I SEE TEACHES ME TO TRUST THE CREATOR FOR ALL I HAVE NOT SEEN

Rating: 1   2   3   4   5   Date Used:

12.

GAMBLING IS THE CHILD OF AVARICE THE BROTHER OF INIQUITY THE FATHER OF MISCHIEF

Rating: 1   2   3   4   5   Date Used:

13.

HE IS HAPPIEST BE HE KING OR PEASANT WHO FINDS PEACE IN HIS HOME—GOETHE

Rating: 1   2   3   4   5   Date Used:

14.

HUMILITY IS THE SOLID FOUNDATION OF ALL THE VIRTUES —CONFUCIUS

Rating: 1   2   3   4   5   Date Used:

15.

WHEREVER THERE IS A HUMAN BEING THERE IS THE OPPORTUNITY FOR KINDNESS

Rating: 1   2   3   4   5   Date Used:

16.

**THE CHRISTIAN LIFE
CONSISTS IN FAITH
AND CHARITY
—LUTHER**

Rating: 1   2   3   4   5   Date Used:

17.

**GOOD LUCK IS A
LAZY MAN'S ESTIMATE
OF A WORKER'S
SUCCESS**

Rating: 1   2   3   4   5   Date Used:

18.

**GOD SEES US AS
WE CAN BE BUT
LOVES US AS WE ARE**

Rating: 1   2   3   4   5   Date Used:

19.

**MONEY IS NOT
REQUIRED TO BUY
THE NECESSITY
OF THE SOUL—THOREAU**

Rating: 1   2   3   4   5   Date Used:

20.

**THOSE WHO NEVER
RETRACT OPINIONS
LOVE THEMSELVES
MORE THAN THE TRUTH**

Rating: 1   2   3   4   5   Date Used:

21.

**PEOPLE SEE GOD
EVERY DAY
THEY JUST DO NOT
RECOGNIZE HIM**

Rating: 1   2   3   4   5   Date Used:

22.

CAMELS AND CHRISTIANS
RELEASE THEIR BURDENS
ON THEIR KNEES

Rating: 1   2   3   4   5   Date Used:

23.

TO PITY DISTRESS
IS HUMAN
TO RELIEVE IT
IS GODLIKE

Rating: 1   2   3   4   5   Date Used:

24.

THE CROSS IS THE
ONLY LADDER HIGH
ENOUGH TO REACH
HEAVEN

Rating: 1   2   3   4   5   Date Used:

25.

WEALTH TASTE AND
LEISURE BRING MANY
THINGS BUT NOT
HAPPINESS—CHURCHILL

Rating: 1   2   3   4   5   Date Used:

26.

THE ONLY PEOPLE
WHO LIKE CHANGE
ARE WET BABIES

Rating: 1   2   3   4   5   Date Used:

27.

TROUBLE OFTEN
STARTS OUT AS
FUN

Rating: 1   2   3   4   5   Date Used:

JOY SOMETIMES
NEEDS PAIN
TO GIVE IT BIRTH

Rating: 1 2 3 4 5 Date Used:

29.

THE TEN COMMANDMENTS
ARE NOT MULTIPLE
CHOICE

Rating: 1 2 3 4 5 Date Used:

30.

A MAN'S TREATMENT
OF MONEY IS THE
MOST DECISIVE TEST
OF HIS CHARACTER

Rating: 1 2 3 4 5 Date Used:

31.

A CHURCH THAT DOES
NOT EVANGELIZE
WILL FOSSILIZE

Rating: 1 2 3 4 5 Date Used:

32.

NEWS FLASH TO
RACISTS FROM GOD
"HEAVEN IS INTEGRATED"

Rating: 1 2 3 4 5 Date Used:

33.

WORDS CAN'T BREAK
BONES BUT THEY CAN
BREAK HEARTS

Rating: 1 2 3 4 5 Date Used:

34.

SORROW LOOKS BACK
WORRY LOOKS AROUND
FAITH LOOKS UP

Rating: 1   2   3   4   5   Date Used:

35.

USE SELF-CONTROL
WITH YOUR REMOTE
CONTROL

Rating: 1   2   3   4   5   Date Used:

36.

LIVE AS IF GOD
SEES AND HEARS
EVERYTHING
BECAUSE HE DOES

Rating: 1   2   3   4   5   Date Used:

37.

A STAR BASEBALL
PLAYER FAILS 70%
OF THE TIME—DO NOT
LET FAILURE STOP YOU

Rating: 1   2   3   4   5   Date Used:

38.

HOPE SPRINGS ETERNAL
WHEN OUR HOPE IS
ETERNAL

Rating: 1   2   3   4   5   Date Used:

39.

HEAVEN—DON'T
MISS IT FOR THE
WORLD

Rating: 1   2   3   4   5   Date Used:

40.

IF YOU CAN'T SLEEP DON'T COUNT SHEEP TALK TO THE SHEPHERD

Rating: 1 2 3 4 5   Date Used:

41.

GIVE YOURSELF TO GOD AND ALL OTHER GIVING IS FUN

Rating: 1 2 3 4 5   Date Used:

42.

MANY PEOPLE WANT TO SERVE GOD BUT ONLY AS ADVISERS

Rating: 1 2 3 4 5   Date Used:

43.

A BIBLE THAT IS FALLING APART OFTEN BELONGS TO SOMEONE WHO ISN'T

Rating: 1 2 3 4 5   Date Used:

44.

A CHURCH THAT WANTS A BETTER PASTOR CAN GET ONE BY PRAYING FOR HIM

Rating: 1 2 3 4 5   Date Used:

45.

THE ROAD TO HELL IS PAVED WITH GOOD TEMPTATIONS

Rating: 1 2 3 4 5   Date Used:

46.

PEACE STARTS WITH A SMILE —MOTHER TERESA

Rating: 1   2   3   4   5   Date Used:

47.

FOR FAST-ACTING RELIEF TRY SLOWING DOWN

Rating: 1   2   3   4   5   Date Used:

48.

TO LOVE AND BE LOVED IS TO FEEL THE SUN FROM BOTH SIDES

Rating: 1   2   3   4   5   Date Used:

49.

THE BEST WAY TO WIN AN ARGUMENT IS TO START BY BEING RIGHT

Rating: 1   2   3   4   5   Date Used:

50.

BELIEVING THE BEST OF OTHERS SAVES SO MUCH TIME

Rating: 1   2   3   4   5   Date Used:

51.

TEACHING KIDS TO COUNT IS GOOD BUT TEACHING THEM WHAT COUNTS IS BEST

Rating: 1   2   3   4   5   Date Used:

52.

EXPERIENCE IS THE NAME EVERYONE GIVES THEIR MISTAKES

Rating: 1 2 3 4 5 Date Used:

53.

WISE MEN GIVE GIFTS OF GOLD FRANKINCENSE AND MIRTH

Rating: 1 2 3 4 5 Date Used:

54.

CHILDREN NEED PARENTS' PRESENCE MORE THAN THEIR PRESENTS

Rating: 1 2 3 4 5 Date Used:

55.

IT IS VERY DANGEROUS TO REASON AND DECIDE WITH INSUFFICIENT DATA

Rating: 1 2 3 4 5 Date Used:

56.

IF JESUS IS NOT LORD OF EVERYTHING IN YOUR LIFE HE IS NOT LORD AT ALL

Rating: 1 2 3 4 5 Date Used:

57.

XMAS IS CHRISTMAS WITHOUT CHRIST DON'T X HIM OUT

Rating: 1 2 3 4 5 Date Used:

58.

A GOOD CONSCIENCE
IS A CONTINUAL
CHRISTMAS
—BEN FRANKLIN

Rating: 1   2   3   4   5   Date Used:

59.

THE TOMB IS EMPTY
JESUS LIVES!
THANK GOD

Rating: 1   2   3   4   5   Date Used:

60.

GOD HAS BLESSED
AMERICA
LET AMERICA
BLESS GOD!

Rating: 1   2   3   4   5   Date Used:

61.

MAY YOUR TROUBLES
LAST AS LONG AS
YOUR NEW YEAR'S
RESOLUTIONS

Rating: 1   2   3   4   5   Date Used:

62.

A HUMBLE MIND IS
THE SOIL FROM WHICH
THANKSGIVING SPRINGS

Rating: 1   2   3   4   5   Date Used:

63.

IF YOU ARE NOT
ASKING GOD FOR
FORGIVENESS
YOU'RE ASKING FOR IT

Rating: 1   2   3   4   5   Date Used:

64.

GOD HAD A PURPOSE
FOR YOU BEFORE
YOU WERE BORN

Rating: 1   2   3   4   5   Date Used:

65.

YOU ARE THE
YARDSTICK BY WHICH
YOUR CHILD DETERMINES
HER SELF-WORTH

Rating: 1   2   3   4   5   Date Used:

66.

WITHIN A THANKFUL
HEART THERE IS NO
ROOM FOR BITTERNESS

Rating: 1   2   3   4   5   Date Used:

67.

JESUS LOVES THE LITTLE
CHILDREN OF THE WORLD:
RED AND YELLOW, BLACK
AND WHITE, AND UNBORN

Rating: 1   2   3   4   5   Date Used:

68.

COMPASSION IN
DEFENSE OF SIN
IS NO VIRTUE

Rating: 1   2   3   4   5   Date Used:

69.

THANKSGIVING IS
THE LANGUAGE
OF HEAVEN

Rating: 1   2   3   4   5   Date Used:

70.

THEY THAT SEEK GOD
IN EVERYTHING
WILL FIND GOD IN
EVERYTHING

Rating: 1 2 3 4 5 Date Used:

71.

THE VICTIM OF THE
CROSS BECAME
THE VICTOR OVER
SIN AND DEATH

Rating: 1 2 3 4 5 Date Used:

72.

A BUDGET HELPS US
TO LIVE BELOW
OUR YEARNINGS

Rating: 1 2 3 4 5 Date Used:

73.

YOU CAN SAVE MONEY
BUT MONEY CAN'T
SAVE YOU

Rating: 1 2 3 4 5 Date Used:

74.

SATAN ALWAYS USES
A LURE
DON'T TAKE THE BAIT

Rating: 1 2 3 4 5 Date Used:

75.

GOD'S ANSWERS
ARE OFTEN BETTER
THAN OUR PRAYERS

Rating: 1 2 3 4 5 Date Used:

76.

THE BEST INVESTMENTS YIELD ETERNAL DIVIDENDS

Rating: 1 2 3 4 5   Date Used:

77.

BEWARE OF THOSE WHO GIVE ADVICE ACCORDING TO THEIR OWN INTERESTS

Rating: 1 2 3 4 5   Date Used:

78.

AN ATHEIST IS A PERSON WITH NO VISIBLE MEANS OF SUPPORT

Rating: 1 2 3 4 5   Date Used:

79.

ALL MORTALS TEND TO TURN INTO THE THING THEY PRETEND TO BE
—C. S. LEWIS

Rating: 1 2 3 4 5   Date Used:

80.

GOD'S IN HIS HEAVEN ALL'S RIGHT WITH THE WORLD
—ROBERT BROWNING

Rating: 1 2 3 4 5   Date Used:

81.

THE SAFEST ROAD TO HELL IS THE GRADUAL ONE, SOFT UNDER FOOT
—C. S. LEWIS

Rating: 1 2 3 4 5   Date Used:

82.

**NO SOMBER GOD
COULD HAVE MADE
A MONKEY, A CAMEL,
AND A GIRAFFE**

Rating: 1   2   3   4   5   Date Used:

83.

**SCIENCE WITHOUT
RELIGION IS LAME
RELIGION WITHOUT
SCIENCE IS BLIND**

Rating: 1   2   3   4   5   Date Used:

84.

**PITY THE POOR ATHEIST
WHO IS GRATEFUL
AND HAS NO ONE
TO THANK**

Rating: 1   2   3   4   5   Date Used:

85.

**YOU CANNOT GET
EYE STRAIN FROM
LOOKING ON THE
BRIGHT SIDE OF THINGS**

Rating: 1   2   3   4   5   Date Used:

86.

**WE TAKE 2 YEARS
TO LEARN TO TALK
AND 60 YEARS TO LEARN
WHEN TO SHUT UP**

Rating: 1   2   3   4   5   Date Used:

87.

**EVERY PERSON HAS AN
EQUAL CHANCE TO
BECOME BETTER
THAN THEY ARE**

Rating: 1   2   3   4   5   Date Used:

88.

**YOU DO NOT SEE
THE THISTLES IN
GREEN GRASS
FROM A DISTANCE**

Rating: 1 2 3 4 5 Date Used:

89.

**WHAT WE SEE OFTEN
DEPENDS ON WHAT WE
ARE LOOKING FOR**

Rating: 1 2 3 4 5 Date Used:

90.

**DIFFICULTIES
MASTERED ARE
OPPORTUNITIES WON
—WINSTON CHURCHILL**

Rating: 1 2 3 4 5 Date Used:

91.

**THE GREAT HOPE OF
SOCIETY IS INDIVIDUAL
CHARACTER
—CHANNING**

Rating: 1 2 3 4 5 Date Used:

92.

**HE WHO BELIEVES IN
NOBODY KNOWS HE
HIMSELF CANNOT BE
TRUSTED**

Rating: 1 2 3 4 5 Date Used:

93.

**THERE IS NO PILLOW
AS SOFT AS A
CLEAR CONSCIENCE**

Rating: 1 2 3 4 5 Date Used:

94.

JESUS:
DON'T LEAVE EARTH
WITHOUT HIM!

Rating: 1 2 3 4 5   Date Used:

95.

BEWARE OF LITTLE
EXPENSES, A SMALL
LEAK WILL SINK A
SHIP—BEN FRANKLIN

Rating: 1 2 3 4 5   Date Used:

96.

COMPANIONSHIP IS
TWO HEARTS
TUGGING AT THE
SAME LOAD

Rating: 1 2 3 4 5   Date Used:

97.

FAMILY IS
MORE SACRED
THAN THE STATE
—POPE PIUS XI

Rating: 1 2 3 4 5   Date Used:

98.

FAITH IS TO BELIEVE
WHAT WE DO NOT SEE
FAITH'S REWARD IS TO
SEE WHAT WE BELIEVE

Rating: 1 2 3 4 5   Date Used:

99.

THE FOOL THINKS HE
IS WISE, BUT THE WISE
MAN KNOWS HE IS A
FOOL—SHAKESPEARE

Rating: 1 2 3 4 5   Date Used:

100.

THE BEST ANTIDOTE
FOR DESPAIR IS TO
DO SOMETHING
FOR SOMEONE

Rating: 1   2   3   4   5   Date Used:

101.

LOST TIME IS
NEVER FOUND AGAIN

Rating: 1   2   3   4   5   Date Used:

102.

KINDNESS IS THE
GOLDEN CHAIN BY
WHICH SOCIETY IS
HELD TOGETHER

Rating: 1   2   3   4   5   Date Used:

103.

GOD AND YOU
CAN OVERCOME
ANYTHING

Rating: 1   2   3   4   5   Date Used:

104.

COME TO CHURCH
AND GET A
FAITH LIFT

Rating: 1   2   3   4   5   Date Used:

105.

A CYNIC KNOWS
THE PRICE OF
EVERYTHING AND THE
VALUE OF NOTHING

Rating: 1   2   3   4   5   Date Used:

106.

THE MORALITY OF THE BIBLE IS THE SAFETY OF SOCIETY
—F. C. MONTFORT

Rating: 1   2   3   4   5   Date Used:

107.

A TREE WILL NOT ONLY LIE AS IT FALLS BUT IT WILL FALL AS IT LEANS

Rating: 1   2   3   4   5   Date Used:

108.

VIRTUE WITH TIMIDITY IS NO MATCH FOR ARMED AND RESOLUTE WICKEDNESS

Rating: 1   2   3   4   5   Date Used:

109.

GOD IS NOT LIMITED BY YOUR CIRCUMSTANCES

Rating: 1   2   3   4   5   Date Used:

110.

GOD IS UP TO SOMETHING GOOD

Rating: 1   2   3   4   5   Date Used:

111.

DUSTY BIBLES LEAD TO DIRTY LIVES

Rating: 1   2   3   4   5   Date Used:

112.   **THE BEAUTY OF
NATURE IS GOD'S
GREETING CARD**

Rating: 1   2   3   4   5   Date Used:

113.   **PATIENCE IS
TRUSTING IN GOD'S
TIMING**

Rating: 1   2   3   4   5   Date Used:

114.   **A SHORTCUT IS
OFTEN TEMPTATION
IN DISGUISE**

Rating: 1   2   3   4   5   Date Used:

115.   **A HUMBLE PERSON
SERVING GOD IS
GREATER THAN A FAMOUS
ONE WHO IS NOT**

Rating: 1   2   3   4   5   Date Used:

116.   **COME JOIN OUR
PROPHET-SHARING
PROGRAM**

Rating: 1   2   3   4   5   Date Used:

117.   **GIVING IS THE ONLY
PROOF GREED HAS
NOT CONSUMED
YOUR SOUL**

Rating: 1   2   3   4   5   Date Used:

118.

NO HEART IS ABANDONED WHOSE TENANT IS JESUS CHRIST

Rating: 1   2   3   4   5   Date Used:

119.

PEOPLE WHO SING THEIR OWN PRAISES HAVE NO ACCOMPANIMENT

Rating: 1   2   3   4   5   Date Used:

120.

WE ARE NOT SAVED BY GOOD WORKS BUT FOR GOOD WORKS

Rating: 1   2   3   4   5   Date Used:

121.

GOD IS LIKE BLEACH HE REMOVES STAINS NO ONE ELSE CAN

Rating: 1   2   3   4   5   Date Used:

122.

SOME THINK THEY ARE BUSY WHEN THEY ARE ONLY CONFUSED

Rating: 1   2   3   4   5   Date Used:

123.

WHEN YOU ARE THROUGH IMPROVING YOU ARE THROUGH

Rating: 1   2   3   4   5   Date Used:

124.   **HE WHO HAS THE
FAITH HAS THE FUN
—G. K. CHESTERTON**

Rating: 1   2   3   4   5   Date Used:

125.   **AN EGOTIST IS
SOMEONE WHO IS
ALWAYS ME-DEEP
IN CONVERSATION**

Rating: 1   2   3   4   5   Date Used:

126.   **COME TO OUR COFFEE
HOUR AND THIRST
AFTER RIGHTEOUSNESS**

Rating: 1   2   3   4   5   Date Used:

127.   **WALKING WITH GOD
IS FAR BETTER THAN
RIDING IN A LIMOUSINE
WITHOUT HIM**

Rating: 1   2   3   4   5   Date Used:

128.   **TO ERR IS HUMAN
TO BLAME IT ON
SOMEONE ELSE IS
EVEN MORE HUMAN**

Rating: 1   2   3   4   5   Date Used:

129.   **SOME MINDS ARE
LIKE CONCRETE
ALL MIXED UP AND
PERMANENTLY SET**

Rating: 1   2   3   4   5   Date Used:

130. **NO ONE IS A FAILURE
WHO LIGHTENS THE
BURDEN OF ANOTHER**

Rating: 1 2 3 4 5 Date Used:

131. **HOSPITALITY IS
MAKING YOUR GUESTS
FEEL AT HOME WHEN
YOU WISH THEY WERE**

Rating: 1 2 3 4 5 Date Used:

132. **SPRING IS GOD'S
WAY OF SAYING HE
LOVES US**

Rating: 1 2 3 4 5 Date Used:

133. **TOMORROW IS THE
BUSIEST DAY OF
THE WEEK**

Rating: 1 2 3 4 5 Date Used:

134. **THERE IS NO SPEED
LIMIT IN THE PURSUIT
OF EXCELLENCE**

Rating: 1 2 3 4 5 Date Used:

135. **GOD'S QUARREL IS
NOT WITH MATERIAL
GOODS BUT WITH
MATERIAL GODS**

Rating: 1 2 3 4 5 Date Used:

136.

HE DIED THAT WE MIGHT HAVE ETERNAL LIFE

Rating: 1 2 3 4 5 Date Used:

137.

EQUAL RIGHTS FOR ALL SPECIAL PRIVILEGES FOR NONE—T. JEFFERSON

Rating: 1 2 3 4 5 Date Used:

138.

THE TOMB IS EMPTY SO YOU DON'T HAVE TO BE

Rating: 1 2 3 4 5 Date Used:

139.

IN THE COOKIES OF LIFE FRIENDS ARE THE CHOCOLATE CHIPS

Rating: 1 2 3 4 5 Date Used:

140.

THE BIBLE IS THE SECOND BEST GIFT GOD HAS EVER GIVEN US

Rating: 1 2 3 4 5 Date Used:

141.

THERE IS NO PEACE OF ANY KIND UNLESS THERE IS FIRST PEACE WITH GOD

Rating: 1 2 3 4 5 Date Used:

142.

**THE MORE YOU TRUST
GOD THE MORE YOU
FIND HE IS FAITHFUL**

Rating: 1   2   3   4   5   Date Used:

143.

**GOD SATISFIES THE
RESTLESSNESS OF THE
HUMAN HEART**

Rating: 1   2   3   4   5   Date Used:

144.

**WARNING: EATING
THE FOOD OF GOD'S
WORD WILL CAUSE
SPIRITUAL GROWTH**

Rating: 1   2   3   4   5   Date Used:

145.

**FORGIVENESS IS NEVER
COMPLETE UNTIL WE
ARE ABLE TO
FORGIVE OURSELVES**

Rating: 1   2   3   4   5   Date Used:

146.

**A PESSIMIST IS A
PERSON WHO NEEDS
A SWIFT KICK IN THEIR
CANT'S**

Rating: 1   2   3   4   5   Date Used:

147.

**DEATH TO THE
CHRISTIAN IS A
TRANSFER TO THE
HOME OFFICE**

Rating: 1   2   3   4   5   Date Used:

148.

A MAN WHO ACTS LIKE A CHILD FORCES HIS WIFE TO BE HIS MOTHER

Rating: 1   2   3   4   5   Date Used:

149.

YESTERDAY AND TOMORROW ARE THIEVES OF TODAY

Rating: 1   2   3   4   5   Date Used:

150.

DRINKING DOESN'T DROWN SORROWS IT IRRIGATES THEM

Rating: 1   2   3   4   5   Date Used:

151.

YOUTH AND BEAUTY FADE BUT CHARACTER IS ETERNAL

Rating: 1   2   3   4   5   Date Used:

152.

ANGER IS ONE LETTER AWAY FROM DANGER

Rating: 1   2   3   4   5   Date Used:

153.

GOD FORMED SIN DEFORMED CHRIST TRANSFORMED

Rating: 1   2   3   4   5   Date Used:

154.

THEY STAND BEST WHO KNEEL MOST

Rating: 1   2   3   4   5   Date Used:

155.

**ANGELS CAN FLY
BECAUSE THEY TAKE
THEMSELVES LIGHTLY
—G. K. CHESTERTON**

Rating: 1 2 3 4 5 Date Used:

156.

**WE OURSELVES
ARE GOD'S TRUE
TEMPLES
—JOHN CALVIN**

Rating: 1 2 3 4 5 Date Used:

157.

**1000 HACK AT THE
BRANCHES OF EVIL
FOR EVERY ONE WHO
STRIKES AT THE ROOT**

Rating: 1 2 3 4 5 Date Used:

158.

**SHORT IS THE WAY
FROM NEED TO
GREED**

Rating: 1 2 3 4 5 Date Used:

159.

**LOVE IS THE ONLY
FORCE CAPABLE OF
MAKING AN ENEMY
A FRIEND—M. L. KING JR.**

Rating: 1 2 3 4 5 Date Used:

160.

**MUSIC IS THE GIFT
OF GOD—I PLACE IT
NEXT TO THEOLOGY
—MARTIN LUTHER**

Rating: 1 2 3 4 5 Date Used:

161.
BEYOND THE TOMB'S OPEN DOOR IS THE LIGHT OF ETERNITY

Rating: 1 2 3 4 5   Date Used:

162.
TRUST IN GOD BUT LOCK YOUR CAR

Rating: 1 2 3 4 5   Date Used:

163.
LAUGH AT HONOR AND YOU WILL GROW TRAITORS

Rating: 1 2 3 4 5   Date Used:

164.
CHRIST IS THE SOLE SOLUTION FOR SOUL POLLUTION

Rating: 1 2 3 4 5   Date Used:

165.
ANXIETY IS UNBELIEF IN DISGUISE

Rating: 1 2 3 4 5   Date Used:

166.
YOU DON'T HAVE TO STOP BREATHING TO DIE

Rating: 1 2 3 4 5   Date Used:

167.
IF YOU THINK YOU DON'T NEED THE CHURCH, YOU INSULT THE FOUNDER

Rating: 1 2 3 4 5   Date Used:

168.

CH _ _ CH
WHAT'S MISSING?
U R

Rating: 1   2   3   4   5   Date Used:

169.

LIFE IS HARD BY
THE YARD BUT A
CINCH BY THE INCH

Rating: 1   2   3   4   5   Date Used:

170.

THE KEY TO FAILURE
IS TRYING TO
PLEASE EVERYBODY

Rating: 1   2   3   4   5   Date Used:

171.

IT IS HARDER TO
CONCEAL IGNORANCE
THAN TO ACQUIRE
KNOWLEDGE

Rating: 1   2   3   4   5   Date Used:

172.

DON'T WAIT FOR THE
HEARSE TO TAKE YOU
TO CHURCH

Rating: 1   2   3   4   5   Date Used:

173.

THOSE WHO STAND
FOR NOTHING FALL
FOR ANYTHING

Rating: 1   2   3   4   5   Date Used:

174. **TEACHERS AFFECT ETERNITY—THEY NEVER KNOW WHERE THEIR INFLUENCE STOPS**

Rating: 1 2 3 4 5 Date Used:

175. **THE MIND IS NOT A VESSEL TO BE FILLED BUT A FIRE TO BE IGNITED—PLUTARCH**

Rating: 1 2 3 4 5 Date Used:

176. **AN HONEST MAN IS THE NOBLEST WORK OF GOD —ROBERT BURNS**

Rating: 1 2 3 4 5 Date Used:

177. **KNOWLEDGE IS POWER —FRANCIS BACON**

Rating: 1 2 3 4 5 Date Used:

178. **MORE THINGS ARE WROUGHT BY PRAYER THAN THE WORLD DREAMS OF—TENNYSON**

Rating: 1 2 3 4 5 Date Used:

179. **A MOTHER'S LOVE IS JUST A SAMPLE OF GOD'S LOVE FOR US**

Rating: 1 2 3 4 5 Date Used:

180. **MOTHER IS ANOTHER NAME FOR LOVE**

Rating: 1 2 3 4 5 Date Used:

181. **GOD COULDN'T BE EVERYWHERE SO HE MADE MOTHERS**

Rating: 1 2 3 4 5 Date Used:

182. **WORRY IS THE THIEF OF JOY**

Rating: 1 2 3 4 5 Date Used:

183. **ALL THAT IS NOT ETERNAL IS ETERNALLY OUT OF DATE—C. S. LEWIS**

Rating: 1 2 3 4 5 Date Used:

184. **SALVATION IS GOD'S ETERNAL PURPOSE FOR YOUR LIFE**

Rating: 1 2 3 4 5 Date Used:

185. **CORRECTION DOES MUCH, BUT ENCOURAGEMENT DOES MORE**

Rating: 1 2 3 4 5 Date Used:

186. **TO HEAR GOD'S VOICE WE NEED TO TURN DOWN THE NOISE OF OF THE WORLD**

Rating: 1 2 3 4 5 Date Used:

187.

LIFE IN CHRIST
IS ALL ABOUT
LIVING LIFE TO
THE FULLEST

Rating: 1   2   3   4   5   Date Used:

188.

IN THE MIDST OF
THE STORM LOOK
FOR CHRIST TO
COME TO YOU

Rating: 1   2   3   4   5   Date Used:

189.

CHRIST WILL NEVER
LEAVE ONE HE HAS
CHOSEN AS HIS OWN

Rating: 1   2   3   4   5   Date Used:

190.

WE WON'T BURN OUT
IF OUR ENERGY COMES
FROM GOD'S SOURCE

Rating: 1   2   3   4   5   Date Used:

191.

BLAMING OTHERS ONLY
DELAYS THE OPERATION
OF GOD'S GRACE IN
YOUR OWN LIFE

Rating: 1   2   3   4   5   Date Used:

192.

WHY CONTINUE TO
CONDEMN YOURSELF
WHEN GOD HAS
FORGIVEN YOU?

Rating: 1   2   3   4   5   Date Used:

193.
DIFFICULTIES MOLD US INTO CHRIST'S LIKENESS AND REVEAL WHO WE ARE

Rating: 1   2   3   4   5   Date Used:

194.
THE LAW TELLS ME HOW CROOKED I AM —GRACE STRAIGHTENS ME OUT

Rating: 1   2   3   4   5   Date Used:

195.
THE MOTIVE BEHIND WHAT YOU PRAY IS AS IMPORTANT AS WHAT YOU ASK FOR

Rating: 1   2   3   4   5   Date Used:

196.
LIFE ISN'T SPINNING OUT OF CONTROL YOU'RE JUST ON GOD'S POTTER'S WHEEL

Rating: 1   2   3   4   5   Date Used:

197.
MOLE HILLS ARE MADE INTO MOUNTAINS BY ADDING DIRT

Rating: 1   2   3   4   5   Date Used:

198.
SMILE—IT MAKES PEOPLE WONDER WHAT YOU ARE UP TO

Rating: 1   2   3   4   5   Date Used:

199.

THE RIGHT TRAIN OF THOUGHT CAN TAKE YOU TO A BETTER STATION IN LIFE

Rating:　　1　2　3　4　5　　　　　Date Used:

200.

A WISE MAN KNOWS IF HE IS FIGHTING FOR A PRINCIPLE OR A PREJUDICE

Rating:　　1　2　3　4　5　　　　　Date Used:

201.

FAILURE IS THE PATH OF LEAST PERSISTENCE

Rating:　　1　2　3　4　5　　　　　Date Used:

202.

YOU HAVE TO BE LITTLE TO BELITTLE

Rating:　　1　2　3　4　5　　　　　Date Used:

203.

TODAY IS THE TOMORROW YOU WORRIED ABOUT YESTERDAY

Rating:　　1　2　3　4　5　　　　　Date Used:

204.

SMALLNESS NEVER KEPT A MOSQUITO FROM BEING EFFECTIVE

Rating:　　1　2　3　4　5　　　　　Date Used:

205.

**YOU AND GOD
ARE A MAJORITY**

Rating: 1   2   3   4   5   Date Used:

206.

**THE GREATEST
TREASON IS TO DO
A RIGHT DEED FOR
THE WRONG REASON**

Rating: 1   2   3   4   5   Date Used:

207.

**SIN NEVER COMES
WRAPPED AS SIN**

Rating: 1   2   3   4   5   Date Used:

208.

**THE HOLY SCRIPTURES
ARE OUR LETTERS
FROM HOME
—ST. AUGUSTINE**

Rating: 1   2   3   4   5   Date Used:

209.

**AN APPLE AND A
HUG A DAY
KEEP THE DOCTOR
AWAY**

Rating: 1   2   3   4   5   Date Used:

210.

**LIE ONCE AND
1000 TRUTHS
WILL BE DOUBTED**

Rating: 1   2   3   4   5   Date Used:

211. **DO YOUR BEST AND LET GOD DO THE REST**

Rating: 1 2 3 4 5 Date Used:

212. **HOPE TIES US TO THE FUTURE AS MEMORY TIES US TO THE PAST**

Rating: 1 2 3 4 5 Date Used:

213. **FEAR IS THE DARKROOM WHERE NEGATIVES ARE DEVELOPED**

Rating: 1 2 3 4 5 Date Used:

214. **GIVE YOURSELF TO GOD AND GIVING TO OTHERS WILL BE EASY AND JOYFUL**

Rating: 1 2 3 4 5 Date Used:

215. **YOU CAN BE RICH BY GETTING MORE OR BY WANTING LESS**

Rating: 1 2 3 4 5 Date Used:

216. **PLAN AHEAD— IT WASN'T RAINING WHEN NOAH BUILT THE ARK**

Rating: 1 2 3 4 5 Date Used:

217.

**PROGRESS INVOLVES
RISKS—YOU CAN'T
STEAL SECOND WITH
YOUR FOOT ON FIRST**

Rating: 1   2   3   4   5   Date Used:

218.

**DO NOT RESENT
GROWING OLD
MANY ARE DENIED
THE PLEASURE**

Rating: 1   2   3   4   5   Date Used:

219.

**WE MAKE A LIVING
BY WHAT WE GET
WE MAKE A LIFE
BY WHAT WE GIVE**

Rating: 1   2   3   4   5   Date Used:

220.

**PREACH THE GOSPEL
AT ALL TIMES . . .
IF NECESSARY
USE WORDS**

Rating: 1   2   3   4   5   Date Used:

221.

**GOD'S SPEAKING
ARE YOU LISTENING?**

Rating: 1   2   3   4   5   Date Used:

222.

**YOU FAIL 100% OF
THE TIME ON RISKS
YOU DO NOT TAKE**

Rating: 1   2   3   4   5   Date Used:

223.   **LIFE IS LIKE TENNIS
                           SERVE WELL AND
                           YOU WILL WIN**

Rating: 1   2   3   4   5   Date Used:

224.   **THERE CAN BE NO
                           MORALITY APART
                           FROM RELIGION**

Rating: 1   2   3   4   5   Date Used:

225.   **GOD'S POTTER'S
                           WHEEL TURNS OUT
                           SAINTS**

Rating: 1   2   3   4   5   Date Used:

226.   **HUMILITY IS TO MAKE
                           A RIGHT ESTIMATE
                           OF ONE'S SELF
                           —C. H. SPURGEON**

Rating: 1   2   3   4   5   Date Used:

227.   **WITHOUT THE CROSS
                           EVEN GOD COULDN'T
                           GIVE US A SECOND
                           CHANCE**

Rating: 1   2   3   4   5   Date Used:

228.   **TRIALS TEST OUR
                           FAITH AND
                           STRENGTHEN OUR
                           SPIRITS**

Rating: 1   2   3   4   5   Date Used:

229.

LIVE FOR ETERNITY AND YOU WON'T MIND DYING

Rating: 1   2   3   4   5   Date Used:

230.

EARTH HAS NO SORROW THAT HEAVEN CANNOT HEAL

Rating: 1   2   3   4   5   Date Used:

231.

HAVE YOU TRIED OUT YOUR SMILE TODAY?

Rating: 1   2   3   4   5   Date Used:

232.

WHEN YOU KILL TIME YOU MURDER SUCCESS

Rating: 1   2   3   4   5   Date Used:

233.

FOR INWARD PEACE TRY THE UPWARD LOOK

Rating: 1   2   3   4   5   Date Used:

234.

KEEP YOUR TEMPER NOBODY WANTS IT

Rating: 1   2   3   4   5   Date Used:

235.

SOME PEOPLE CARVE CAREERS OTHERS CHISEL

Rating: 1   2   3   4   5   Date Used:

236.

GENIUS BEGINS GREAT WORKS—HARD WORK ALONE FINISHES THEM

Rating: 1 2 3 4 5 Date Used:

237.

IF YOUR KNEES KNOCK KNEEL ON THEM

Rating: 1 2 3 4 5 Date Used:

238.

WHEN SATAN REMINDS YOU OF YOUR PAST REMIND HIM OF HIS FUTURE

Rating: 1 2 3 4 5 Date Used:

239.

SIN ALWAYS HAS AN "I" IN THE MIDDLE

Rating: 1 2 3 4 5 Date Used:

240.

THE 10 COMMANDMENTS ARE NOT A TRAP BUT A MAP

Rating: 1 2 3 4 5 Date Used:

241.

PURITY OF HEART AND SIMPLICITY ARE GREAT FORCES WITH ALMIGHTY GOD

Rating: 1 2 3 4 5 Date Used:

242. **OUR SPEECH GIVES THE BEST VIEW OF WHAT'S IN OUR HEART**

Rating: 1   2   3   4   5   Date Used:

243. **PRAYER IS THE PREFACE TO THE BOOK OF CHRISTIAN LIVING**

Rating: 1   2   3   4   5   Date Used:

244. **FEED YOUR FAITH AND DOUBT WILL STARVE TO DEATH**

Rating: 1   2   3   4   5   Date Used:

245. **THIS IS OUR GREAT NEED—TO BE MORE LIKE CHRIST**

Rating: 1   2   3   4   5   Date Used:

246. **ADVERSITY MAKES US BITTER OR BETTER**

Rating: 1   2   3   4   5   Date Used:

247. **DESPAIR COMES FROM NOT KNOWING THIS IS NOT OUR HOME**

Rating: 1   2   3   4   5   Date Used:

248.   **TOLERANCE OF SIN
IS A VIRTUE TO THOSE
WHO LACK PRINCIPLES**

Rating: 1   2   3   4   5   Date Used:

249.   **THERE ARE ETERNAL
REASONS FOR
TEMPORARY TRIALS**

Rating: 1   2   3   4   5   Date Used:

250.   **A CHRIST-HONORING
LIFE IS FULL OF LOVE,
HUMILITY, AND
INTEGRITY**

Rating: 1   2   3   4   5   Date Used:

251.   **EVERY INORDINATE
AFFECTION HAS ITS
OWN PUNISHMENT**

Rating: 1   2   3   4   5   Date Used:

252.   **CONSTANT PRAYER IS
TO KEEP THE HEART
ALWAYS RIGHT
TOWARD GOD**

Rating: 1   2   3   4   5   Date Used:

253.   **THE HARDER YOU
WORK THE LUCKIER
YOU GET**

Rating: 1   2   3   4   5   Date Used:

254.

HAVE YOU OPENED YOUR BANK ACCOUNT IN HEAVEN?

Rating: 1   2   3   4   5   Date Used:

255.

DEATH HOLDS NO FEAR FOR THE CHILD OF GOD

Rating: 1   2   3   4   5   Date Used:

256.

TRIALS ARE MEDICINES GIVEN BY GOD FOR OUR SPIRITUAL HEALTH

Rating: 1   2   3   4   5   Date Used:

257.

THE KEY TO HEARING GOD'S VOICE IS FOUND IN PRACTICING HIS PRESENCE

Rating: 1   2   3   4   5   Date Used:

258.

GOD'S LOVE SUPERSEDES OUR GREATEST SORROW

Rating: 1   2   3   4   5   Date Used:

259.

DIE TO SELF AND LIVE FOR GOD

Rating: 1   2   3   4   5   Date Used:

260.

**GOD BASES OUR WORTH
NOT ON WHAT WE HAVE
BUT ON WHO WE HAVE
NAMELY JESUS CHRIST**

Rating: 1   2   3   4   5   Date Used:

261.

**FORGIVENESS KILLS
RESENTMENT AND
HATRED, AND REMOVES
SELFISHNESS**

Rating: 1   2   3   4   5   Date Used:

262.

**IN CHRIST WE HAVE
VICTORY FOR EVERY
CHALLENGE WE FACE**

Rating: 1   2   3   4   5   Date Used:

263.

**THE JOY OF GOD
IS ETERNAL**

Rating: 1   2   3   4   5   Date Used:

264.

**JOY IS
FOUNDATIONAL TO
THE CHRISTIAN LIFE**

Rating: 1   2   3   4   5   Date Used:

265.

**THERE IS NO GREATER
GIFT THAN THE GIFT
OF CHRIST'S JOY**

Rating: 1   2   3   4   5   Date Used:

266.

JOY'S RESIDENCE
IS ETERNAL IN THE
CHRISTIAN'S HEART

Rating: 1   2   3   4   5   Date Used:

267.

GOD OFTEN GUIDES
US BY CIRCUMSTANCES

Rating: 1   2   3   4   5   Date Used:

268.

GOD'S LOVE FOR YOU
IS THE GREATEST
REASON TO TURN
FROM SIN

Rating: 1   2   3   4   5   Date Used:

269.

TO BECOME ETERNAL
JOIN YOURSELF TO
THE ETERNAL

Rating: 1   2   3   4   5   Date Used:

270.

FAITH MAKES ALL
THINGS POSSIBLE
LOVE MAKES ALL
THINGS EASY—D. MOODY

Rating: 1   2   3   4   5   Date Used:

271.

NO ACT OF LOVE
IS EVER WASTED

Rating: 1   2   3   4   5   Date Used:

272.   **LOVE YOUR ENEMIES**
                           IT WILL DRIVE
                           THEM NUTS

Rating: 1   2   3   4   5   Date Used:

273.   **GAMBLING IS A SURE**
                         WAY TO GET NOTHING
                         FOR SOMETHING

Rating: 1   2   3   4   5   Date Used:

274.   **THERE IS NO PROGRESS**
                         WITHOUT RESISTANCE

Rating: 1   2   3   4   5   Date Used:

275.   **YOUR SINS LIE**
                           EITHER ON YOU OR
                         ON CHRIST—IF ON YOU
                           YOU'RE LOST

Rating: 1   2   3   4   5   Date Used:

276.   **SPRING REMINDS US**
                         OF THE RESURRECTION
                         IT'S WRITTEN IN EVERY
                         NEW LEAF AND FLOWER

Rating: 1   2   3   4   5   Date Used:

277.   **PRIDE LIES IN WAIT**
                           TO DESTROY
                           GOOD DEEDS

Rating: 1   2   3   4   5   Date Used:

278.

WE GAIN IMMENSE VALUE WHEN WE BELONG TO GOD

Rating: 1 2 3 4 5   Date Used:

279.

GIVE ME THE LOVE THAT LEADS THE WAY THE FAITH THAT NOTHING CAN DISMAY

Rating: 1 2 3 4 5   Date Used:

280.

IF YOU'RE SEPARATED YOU MAY BE USING THE WRONG KIND OF GLUE

Rating: 1 2 3 4 5   Date Used:

281.

LAUGHTER IS ANOTHER WAY OF SAYING I LOVE YOU

Rating: 1 2 3 4 5   Date Used:

282.

A GOOD LAUGH IS SUNSHINE IN A HOUSE

Rating: 1 2 3 4 5   Date Used:

283.

LAUGHTER IS A GIFT WE USE TO DISPLACE DARKNESS

Rating: 1 2 3 4 5   Date Used:

284.

WHOLESOME LAUGHTER
IS A RESURRECTION
OF THE SPIRIT

Rating: 1 2 3 4 5   Date Used:

285.

CHANGE IS INEVITABLE
GROWTH IS OPTIONAL

Rating: 1 2 3 4 5   Date Used:

286.

PROBLEMS ARE
OPPORTUNITIES IN
THEIR WORK CLOTHES

Rating: 1 2 3 4 5   Date Used:

287.

IT IS BETTER TO USE
EXERCISE TO PRESERVE
HEALTH THAN MEDICINE
TO GET IT BACK

Rating: 1 2 3 4 5   Date Used:

288.

GO OUT ON A LIMB
THAT'S WHERE
THE FRUIT IS

Rating: 1 2 3 4 5   Date Used:

289.

WORRY LESS ABOUT
WHAT TO LIVE ON AND
MORE ABOUT WHAT TO
LIVE FOR

Rating: 1 2 3 4 5   Date Used:

290.

**TOO MANY FOLKS
SPEND THEIR LIVES
AGING RATHER
THAN MATURING**

Rating: 1   2   3   4   5   Date Used:

291.

**YOU ARE OLD
WHEN REGRETS TAKE
THE PLACE OF DREAMS**

Rating: 1   2   3   4   5   Date Used:

292.

**DON'T GIVE UNTIL IT
HURTS GIVE UNTIL
IT FEELS GOOD**

Rating: 1   2   3   4   5   Date Used:

293.

**WE CAN'T SUBSTITUTE
THE VIRTUES OF MAN
FOR THE LAW OF GOD**

Rating: 1   2   3   4   5   Date Used:

294.

**BAPTISM IS NOT AN
OPTION IT IS A
DIVINE OPPORTUNITY**

Rating: 1   2   3   4   5   Date Used:

295.

**GOD HONORS A
HEART OF FAITH**

Rating: 1   2   3   4   5   Date Used:

296.

THE RIGHTEOUSNESS OF CHRIST IS THE ROBE OF OUR LIVES

Rating: 1   2   3   4   5   Date Used:

297.

GOD PROMISED A SAFE LANDING NOT AN EASY FLIGHT

Rating: 1   2   3   4   5   Date Used:

298.

ALL CREATED THINGS ARE LIVING IN THE HAND OF GOD

Rating: 1   2   3   4   5   Date Used:

299.

FAITH UNTESTED IS FAITH UNFULFILLED

Rating: 1   2   3   4   5   Date Used:

300.

THE CHRISTIAN LIFE IS A MARATHON THAT BEGINS WITH A WALK

Rating: 1   2   3   4   5   Date Used:

301.

SATAN IS THE FATHER OF LIES HE FLEES FROM THE TRUTH

Rating: 1   2   3   4   5   Date Used:

302.
CONCERNING TEMPTATION GOD ALWAYS MAKES A WAY TO ESCAPE

Rating: 1   2   3   4   5   Date Used:

303.
IF THE MIND CAN CONCEIVE IT THE HEART BELIEVE IT YOU CAN ACHIEVE IT

Rating: 1   2   3   4   5   Date Used:

304.
JESUS IS THE REASON FOR THE SEASON DON'T XMAS HIM OUT

Rating: 1   2   3   4   5   Date Used:

305.
SUCCESS IS FAILURE TURNED INSIDE OUT

Rating: 1   2   3   4   5   Date Used:

306.
IT TAKES A LOT OF FAITH TO BE AN ATHEIST

Rating: 1   2   3   4   5   Date Used:

307.
TAKE A STROLL WITH YOUR SOUL ON YOUR KNEES—PRAY

Rating: 1   2   3   4   5   Date Used:

308.

BE AN ORGAN DONOR
GIVE YOUR HEART TO
JESUS

Rating: 1   2   3   4   5   Date Used:

309.

IF IT IS GOD WE LOVE
OUR HOPE AND
TREASURE LIE ABOVE

Rating: 1   2   3   4   5   Date Used:

310.

DO NOT PRAY FOR A
LIGHTER LOAD BUT
FOR A STRONGER
BACK

Rating: 1   2   3   4   5   Date Used:

311.

WE HAVE A HOUSE ON
HIGH FRAMED
BY THE MIGHTY
ARCHITECT

Rating: 1   2   3   4   5   Date Used:

312.

THE DEVIL IS A BETTER
THEOLOGIAN THAN ANY
OF US, YET IS A DEVIL
STILL—A. W. TOZER

Rating: 1   2   3   4   5   Date Used:

313.

WISDOM IS SEEING
THINGS FROM GOD'S
PERSPECTIVE

Rating: 1   2   3   4   5   Date Used:

314.

LIFE'S GREATEST GIFT IS GOD'S PERSONAL EXPRESSION OF LOVE FOR US

Rating: 1   2   3   4   5   Date Used:

315.

PEOPLE ARE LONELY BECAUSE THEY BUILD WALLS NOT BRIDGES

Rating: 1   2   3   4   5   Date Used:

316.

BETTER TO GIVE LITTLE WITH HUMILITY THAN GREAT TREASURE WITH VANITY

Rating: 1   2   3   4   5   Date Used:

317.

WHEN WE FOCUS ON OURSELVES WE SEE NOTHING ELSE

Rating: 1   2   3   4   5   Date Used:

318.

GIVING IS LIVING TAKING IS NOT

Rating: 1   2   3   4   5   Date Used:

319.

PEOPLE ARE HONORED NOT FOR WHAT THEY TAKE BUT FOR WHAT THEY GIVE

Rating: 1   2   3   4   5   Date Used:

320.   **SOME PEOPLE MISTAKE
A SHORT MEMORY
FOR A CLEAR
CONSCIENCE**

Rating: 1   2   3   4   5   Date Used:

321.   **MARRIAGES MAY BE
MADE IN HEAVEN BUT
THEY ARE MAINTAINED
ON EARTH**

Rating: 1   2   3   4   5   Date Used:

322.   **WHEN YOU FIND
YOURSELF IN A HOLE
STOP DIGGING
—U. S. GRANT**

Rating: 1   2   3   4   5   Date Used:

323.   **A GOD ALL MERCY
IS A GOD UNJUST**

Rating: 1   2   3   4   5   Date Used:

324.   **APATHY IS A GLOVE
INTO WHICH EVIL
SLIPS ITS HAND**

Rating: 1   2   3   4   5   Date Used:

325.   **THE BIBLE IS THE ROCK
ON WHICH THE
REPUBLIC RESTS
—ANDREW JACKSON**

Rating: 1   2   3   4   5   Date Used:

326. **IF YOU RISK NOTHING
YOU RISK EVERYTHING**

Rating: 1 2 3 4 5 Date Used:

327. **MOST PEOPLE FORGET
GOD ALL DAY AND ASK
FORGIVENESS AT NIGHT**

Rating: 1 2 3 4 5 Date Used:

328. **CALL ON GOD BUT ROW
AWAY FROM THE ROCKS**

Rating: 1 2 3 4 5 Date Used:

329. **REASON SAW NOT
UNTIL FAITH TURNED
ON THE LIGHT**

Rating: 1 2 3 4 5 Date Used:

330. **DO NOT LET THE GOOD
THINGS IN LIFE ROB
YOU OF THE BEST**

Rating: 1 2 3 4 5 Date Used:

331. **VALUE IS NOT
MEASURED BY
SERVANTS BUT BY
THOSE SERVED**

Rating: 1 2 3 4 5 Date Used:

332. **THE GREATEST POVERTY
IS POVERTY OF THE SOUL
—IT IS LACK OF GOD**

Rating: 1 2 3 4 5 Date Used:

333.

**THERE IS NEVER ANY
PEACE FOR THOSE
WHO RESIST GOD**

Rating: 1   2   3   4   5   Date Used:

334.

**CHRISTIANS MUST
REMEMBER OUR
MISSION IS FISHIN'**

Rating: 1   2   3   4   5   Date Used:

335.

**IF GOD SEEMS FAR
AWAY—GUESS WHO
MOVED**

Rating: 1   2   3   4   5   Date Used:

336.

**IT IS A HEAVY
RESPONSIBILITY TO
OWN A BIBLE**

Rating: 1   2   3   4   5   Date Used:

337.

**SELF-CENTERED IS
OFF-CENTERED**

Rating: 1   2   3   4   5   Date Used:

338.

**GIVE YOUR TROUBLES
TO GOD HE'LL BE UP
ALL NIGHT ANYWAY**

Rating: 1   2   3   4   5   Date Used:

339.

**ENCOURAGEMENT IS
OXYGEN TO THE SOUL**

Rating: 1   2   3   4   5   Date Used:

340. **YOU CAN GIVE WITHOUT LOVING BUT YOU CAN'T LOVE WITHOUT GIVING**

Rating: 1   2   3   4   5   Date Used:

341. **GOD IS AT THE END OF YOUR ROPE**

Rating: 1   2   3   4   5   Date Used:

342. **WHAT SUNSHINE IS TO FLOWERS SMILES ARE TO PEOPLE**

Rating: 1   2   3   4   5   Date Used:

343. **LOOK AROUND AND BE DISTRESSED LOOK TO JESUS AND BE AT REST**

Rating: 1   2   3   4   5   Date Used:

344. **A GOOD LAUGH IS SUNSHINE TO THE SOUL AND MEDICINE TO THE BODY**

Rating: 1   2   3   4   5   Date Used:

345. **DAILY PRAYERS WILL DIMINISH YOUR CARES**

Rating: 1   2   3   4   5   Date Used:

346. **A GOOD DEED IS NEVER LOST**

Rating: 1   2   3   4   5   Date Used:

347.

**NOTHING BEATS LOVE
AT FIRST SIGHT EXCEPT
LOVE WITH INSIGHT**

Rating: 1 2 3 4 5 Date Used:

348.

**SOW COURTESY
REAP FRIENDSHIP
PLANT KINDNESS
REAP LOVE**

Rating: 1 2 3 4 5 Date Used:

349.

**FORGIVENESS IS GIVING
LOVE WHEN THERE IS
NO REASON TO**

Rating: 1 2 3 4 5 Date Used:

350.

**A HOUSE IS MADE OF
WALLS AND BEAMS
A HOME IS MADE OF
LOVE AND DREAMS**

Rating: 1 2 3 4 5 Date Used:

351.

**EVERYONE HAS
PATIENCE—SUCCESSFUL
PEOPLE LEARN TO USE IT**

Rating: 1 2 3 4 5 Date Used:

352.

**NOTHING IS SO STRONG
AS GENTLENESS—NOTHING
SO GENTLE AS REAL
STRENGTH**

Rating: 1 2 3 4 5 Date Used:

353.

WATCH OUT FOR TEMPTATION—THE MORE YOU SEE OF IT THE BETTER IT LOOKS

Rating: 1   2   3   4   5   Date Used:

354.

LOVE YOUR ENEMIES IT WILL CONFUSE THEM

Rating: 1   2   3   4   5   Date Used:

355.

ANGER IS TEMPORARY INSANITY

Rating: 1   2   3   4   5   Date Used:

356.

IF YOU LOSE YOUR TEMPER DON'T TRY TO FIND IT

Rating: 1   2   3   4   5   Date Used:

357.

GOD WANTS US TO LOSE OUR TEMPERS FOR GOOD

Rating: 1   2   3   4   5   Date Used:

358.

THERE ARE NO DOUBTERS IN HEAVEN OR HELL

Rating: 1   2   3   4   5   Date Used:

359.

SATAN IS NO ATHEIST

Rating: 1   2   3   4   5   Date Used:

360.   **THE HEART OF THE
GOSPEL IS
REDEMPTION
THROUGH CHRIST**

Rating: 1   2   3   4   5   Date Used:

361.   **IF YOU WISH TO
KNOW GOD YOU MUST
KNOW HIS WORD**

Rating: 1   2   3   4   5   Date Used:

362.   **A SERMON OFTEN DOES
MOST GOOD WHEN IT
MAKES US MOST ANGRY**

Rating: 1   2   3   4   5   Date Used:

363.   **NOTHING PROVOKES
THE DEVIL MORE
THAN THE CROSS**

Rating: 1   2   3   4   5   Date Used:

364.   **WE LIVE BETTER
WHEN WE REMEMBER
WE MUST DIE**

Rating: 1   2   3   4   5   Date Used:

365.   **FOR THE CHRISTIAN
TO DIE IS NOT LOSS
BUT ETERNAL GAIN**

Rating: 1   2   3   4   5   Date Used:

366.   **FEAR OF DYING
MAKES FOR FEAR
OF LIVING**

Rating: 1   2   3   4   5   Date Used:

367.   **NOTHING PUTS MORE
LIFE IN PEOPLE THAN
A DYING SAVIOR**

Rating: 1   2   3   4   5   Date Used:

368.   **BE COMFORTED IF THE
DEVIL IS YOUR
ADVERSARY**

Rating: 1   2   3   4   5   Date Used:

369.   **GOD DISCIPLINES
THOSE HE LOVES
WITH LOVE**

Rating: 1   2   3   4   5   Date Used:

370.   **FAITH IS THE SUREST
OF ALL SIN KILLERS**

Rating: 1   2   3   4   5   Date Used:

371.   **A PERSON IS REALLY
POOR WHO NEVER GIVES**

Rating: 1   2   3   4   5   Date Used:

372.   **IN THE GOSPELS ONE
SIZE FITS ALL**

Rating: 1   2   3   4   5   Date Used:

373.

GOD'S HAMMER CAN SMASH THE HARDEST HEART

Rating: 1 2 3 4 5 Date Used:

374.

HYPOCRISY IS A STENCH IN THE NOSTRILS OF GOD AND HUMANKIND

Rating: 1 2 3 4 5 Date Used:

375.

EVERY CHRISTIAN IS EITHER A MISSIONARY OR AN IMPOSTOR —C. H. SPURGEON

Rating: 1 2 3 4 5 Date Used:

376.

TEN MINUTES PRAYING IS BETTER THAN A YEAR'S MURMURING —C. H. SPURGEON

Rating: 1 2 3 4 5 Date Used:

377.

PREACHING IS SOWING PRAYER IS WATERING BUT PRAISE IS THE HARVEST

Rating: 1 2 3 4 5 Date Used:

378.

WHERE 1 HAS BEEN RUINED BY ADVERSITY 10,000 HAVE BEEN RUINED BY PROSPERITY

Rating: 1 2 3 4 5 Date Used:

379.
SELF-RIGHTEOUSNESS IS AS MUCH AN AFFRONT TO GOD AS BLASPHEMY

Rating: 1   2   3   4   5   Date Used:

380.
IN THE RELIGION OF CHRIST THERE IS NO TAXATION, ALL IS OF LOVE—C. H. SPURGEON

Rating: 1   2   3   4   5   Date Used:

381.
GOD HAD ONE SON WITHOUT SIN HE NEVER HAD A SON WITHOUT TRIAL

Rating: 1   2   3   4   5   Date Used:

382.
UNBELIEF WILL DESTROY THE BEST FAITH WILL SAVE THE WORST

Rating: 1   2   3   4   5   Date Used:

383.
FRIENDSHIPS DOUBLE OUR JOY AND DIVIDE OUR GRIEF

Rating: 1   2   3   4.   5   Date Used:

384.
STACK EVERY BIT OF CRITICISM BETWEEN TWO LAYERS OF PRAISE

Rating: 1   2   3   4   5   Date Used:

385.

**COURAGE IS THE
MASTERY OF FEAR
NOT THE ABSENCE
OF FEAR**

Rating: 1   2   3   4   5   Date Used:

386.

**TRIUMPH IS JUST
"UMPH" ADDED
TO TRY**

Rating: 1   2   3   4   5   Date Used:

387.

**GOOD WORKS ARE
WORTH MUCH AND
COST LITTLE**

Rating: 1   2   3   4   5   Date Used:

388.

**THE KEY TO FAILURE
IS TO TRY TO PLEASE
EVERYONE**

Rating: 1   2   3   4   5   Date Used:

389.

**OUR OBLIGATION IS
TO DO THE RIGHT
THING—THE REST IS
UP TO GOD**

Rating: 1   2   3   4   5   Date Used:

390.

**BETTER TO WALK WITH
WITH GOD IN THE DARK
THAN TO GO ALONE IN
THE LIGHT**

Rating: 1   2   3   4   5   Date Used:

391. **REMEMBER THE BANANA—WHEN IT LEFT THE BUNCH IT GOT SKINNED**

Rating: 1 2 3 4 5 Date Used:

392. **OUR CONSCIENCE IS GOD'S BUILT-IN WARNING SYSTEM**

Rating: 1 2 3 4 5 Date Used:

393. **NEVER LET ADVERSITY GET YOU DOWN EXCEPT ON YOUR KNEES**

Rating: 1 2 3 4 5 Date Used:

394. **NO ONE WILL STAND BEFORE GOD IN HEAVEN WHO HASN'T KNELT ON EARTH**

Rating: 1 2 3 4 5 Date Used:

395. **REMEMBER THE TEA KETTLE WHEN IT'S UP TO ITS NECK IN HOT WATER IT STILL SINGS**

Rating: 1 2 3 4 5 Date Used:

396. **THE SECRET TO CONTENTMENT IS TO REALIZE LIFE IS A GIFT NOT A RIGHT**

Rating: 1 2 3 4 5 Date Used:

397.

CONTENTMENT LIES NOT IN GETTING MORE—BUT IN WANTING LESS

Rating: 1 2 3 4 5 Date Used:

398.

IT'S NOT THE OUTLOOK BUT THE UPLOOK THAT COUNTS

Rating: 1 2 3 4 5 Date Used:

399.

FAITH IS DARING THE SOUL TO GO BEYOND WHAT THE EYES CAN SEE

Rating: 1 2 3 4 5 Date Used:

400.

THOSE WHO DESERVE LOVE THE LEAST NEED IT THE MOST

Rating: 1 2 3 4 5 Date Used:

401.

PEOPLE MAY DOUBT WHAT YOU SAY BUT NEVER WHAT YOU DO

Rating: 1 2 3 4 5 Date Used:

402.

KINDNESS IS THE OIL THAT TAKES THE FRICTION OUT OF LIFE

Rating: 1 2 3 4 5 Date Used:

403.

**HUMOR IS TO LIFE
WHAT SHOCK
ABSORBERS ARE
TO CARS**

Rating:　　　1　2　3　4　5　　　　　Date Used:

404.

**JESUS CAN TURN WATER
INTO WINE BUT HE
CAN'T TURN WHINING
INTO ANYTHING**

Rating:　　　1　2　3　4　5　　　　　Date Used:

405.

**KINDNESS IS A
LANGUAGE THE BLIND
CAN SEE AND THE
DEAF CAN HEAR**

Rating:　　　1　2　3　4　5　　　　　Date Used:

406.

**PRAISE IS LIKE GOLD
IT OWES ITS VALUE
TO ITS SCARCITY**

Rating:　　　1　2　3　4　5　　　　　Date Used:s

407.

**PEOPLE WITH TACT
HAVE LESS
TO RETRACT**

Rating:　　　1　2　3　4　5　　　　　Date Used:

408.

**DON'T LET YOUR
FOOTPRINT IN THE
SANDS OF TIME BE
THE MARK OF A HEEL**

Rating:　　　1　2　3　4　5　　　　　Date Used:

409. **FAULTS ARE THICK WHERE LOVE IS THIN**

Rating: 1 2 3 4 5 Date Used:

410. **HONESTY IS THE FIRST CHAPTER IN THE BOOK OF WISDOM**

Rating: 1 2 3 4 5 Date Used:

411. **FAITH IS NOT BELIEF WITHOUT PROOF BUT TRUST WITHOUT RESERVATION**

Rating: 1 2 3 4 5 Date Used:

412. **A DAY HEMMED IN PRAYER IS LESS LIKELY TO UNRAVEL**

Rating: 1 2 3 4 5 Date Used:

413. **WHEN YOU FLEE TEMPTATIONS DON'T LEAVE A FORWARDING ADDRESS**

Rating: 1 2 3 4 5 Date Used:

414. **LAUGHTER IS A TRANQUILIZER WITH NO SIDE EFFECTS**

Rating: 1 2 3 4 5 Date Used:

415.

**GOD ASKS NOT ABOUT
OUR ABILITY OR
INABILITY JUST OUR
AVAILABILITY**

Rating:　　　1　2　3　4　5　　　Date Used:

416.

**IF YOU THINK YOU
CAN OR YOU CAN'T
YOU'RE RIGHT**

Rating:　　　1　2　3　4　5　　　Date Used:

417.

**GOD MEETS US AT
OUR POINT OF
GREATEST NEED**

Rating:　　　1　2　3　4　5　　　Date Used:

418.

**FORGIVENESS IS
GOD'S GIFT TO US
—ST. AUGUSTINE**

Rating:　　　1　2　3　4　5　　　Date Used:

419.

**PRAISE IS APPLAUSE
FOR THE GOD WHO
LOVES YOU AND KEEPS
YOUR SOUL**

Rating:　　　1　2　3　4　5　　　Date Used:

420.

**WITHOUT GOALS WE
JUST DRIFT ABOUT
UNABLE TO CHART OUR
ACHIEVEMENTS**

Rating:　　　1　2　3　4　5　　　Date Used:

421.

THE CONDITION OF AN ENLIGHTENED MIND IS A SURRENDERED HEART

Rating: 1   2   3   4   5   Date Used:

422.

DEBT ENSLAVES THE BORROWER TO THE LENDER

Rating: 1   2   3   4   5   Date Used:

423.

YOU CAN NEVER OUT-GIVE GOD

Rating: 1   2   3   4   5   Date Used:

424.

TEMPTATION IS COMMON TO ALL GIVING IN IS COMMON TO THE WEAK

Rating: 1   2   3   4   5   Date Used:

425.

IT TAKES COURAGE TO BELIEVE WE ARE FORGIVEN

Rating: 1   2   3   4   5   Date Used:

426.

JEALOUSY'S WOUNDS ARE SELF-INFLICTED

Rating: 1   2   3   4   5   Date Used:

427.

REMOVE THE RESURRECTION AND CHRISTIANITY IS DESTROYED

Rating: 1 2 3 4 5 Date Used:

428.

FEAR IS A NATURAL REACTION TO MOVING CLOSER TO THE TRUTH

Rating: 1 2 3 4 5 Date Used:

429.

IT IS EASIER TO ARGUE PRINCIPLES THAN TO LIVE THEM

Rating: 1 2 3 4 5 Date Used:

430.

SALVATION COST GOD DEARLY SO FOR US IT WOULD BE FREE

Rating: 1 2 3 4 5 Date Used:

431.

FAITH IS LIKE MUSCLE IT GROWS STRONGER THROUGH EXERCISE

Rating: 1 2 3 4 5 Date Used:

432.

FAITH: USE IT OR LOSE IT

Rating: 1 2 3 4 5 Date Used:

433.

OUR BOSS IS A JEWISH CARPENTER

Rating: 1 2 3 4 5 Date Used:

434.   **MAKING A LIVING
IS QUITE DIFFERENT
FROM MAKING A LIFE**

Rating: 1   2   3   4   5   Date Used:

435.   **ONE DOESN'T HAVE
TO BE A PAIN JUST
BECAUSE ONE HAS ONE**

Rating: 1   2   3   4   5   Date Used:

436.   **FRIENDS ARE
FOREVER FRIENDS
IN JESUS**

Rating: 1   2   3   4   5   Date Used:

437.   **THE ONLY THING
CHRISTIANS HAVE TO
FEAR IS EVIL—IT
SEPARATES FROM GOD**

Rating: 1   2   3   4   5   Date Used:

438.   **THE SEEDS OF LOVE
ALWAYS PRODUCE A
BUMPER CROP**

Rating: 1   2   3   4   5   Date Used:

439.   **SOW SEEDS OF LOVE
AND GROW RICH**

Rating: 1   2   3   4   5   Date Used:

440.   **FOR SUCCESS—FOLLOW
THE MAKER'S MANUAL
—READ THE BIBLE**

Rating: 1   2   3   4   5   Date Used:

441.

THE BIBLE IS GOD'S OWNER'S MANUAL FOR LIFETIME MAINTENANCE

Rating: 1   2   3   4   5   Date Used:

442.

FREE TRIP TO HEAVEN! DETAILS INSIDE

Rating: 1   2   3   4   5   Date Used:

443.

TRY OUR SUNDAYS THEY'RE BETTER THAN BASKIN ROBBINS

Rating: 1   2   3   4   5   Date Used:

444.

GOD SO LOVED THE WORLD HE DIDN'T SEND A COMMITTEE

Rating: 1   2   3   4   5   Date Used:

445.

WHEN DOWN IN THE MOUTH REMEMBER JONAH—HE CAME OUT ALL RIGHT

Rating: 1   2   3   4   5   Date Used:

446.

FIGHT TRUTH DECAY STUDY THE BIBLE

Rating: 1   2   3   4   5   Date Used:

447.

IT IS UNLIKELY THERE WILL BE A REDUCTION IN THE WAGES OF SIN

Rating: 1   2   3   4   5   Date Used:

448.

IF YOU'RE HEADED IN THE WRONG DIRECTION GOD ALLOWS U-TURNS

Rating: 1   2   3   4   5   Date Used:

449.

IF YOU DON'T LIKE THE WAY YOU WERE BORN—TRY BEING BORN AGAIN

Rating: 1   2   3   4   5   Date Used:

450.

FORBIDDEN FRUIT CREATES MANY JAMS

Rating: 1   2   3   4   5   Date Used:

451.

IN THE DARK? FOLLOW THE SON

Rating: 1   2   3   4   5   Date Used:

452.

RUNNING LOW ON FAITH? STOP IN FOR A FILL-UP

Rating: 1   2   3   4   5   Date Used:

453.

IF YOU THINK THESE MESSAGES ARE GOOD COME HEAR THE ONES INSIDE ON SUNDAYS

Rating: 1   2   3   4   5   Date Used:

454.

COME TO CHURCH THIS SUNDAY—BEAT THE CHRISTMAS AND EASTER CROWDS

Rating:　　1　2　3　4　5　　　　Date Used:

455.

HOW WOULD YOU LIKE YOUR ETERNITY? WITH OR WITHOUT GOD?

Rating:　　1　2　3　4　5　　　　Date Used:

456.

LAZINESS TRAVELS SO SLOWLY POVERTY ALWAYS CATCHES UP

Rating:　　1　2　3　4　5　　　　Date Used:

457.

THEY WHO DO NOT FORGIVE DESTROY THE BRIDGE THEY MUST CROSS

Rating:　　1　2　3　4　5　　　　Date Used:

458.

REGARDING GOD: LUKEWARMNESS IS WORSE THAN UNBELIEF

Rating:　　1　2　3　4　5　　　　Date Used:

459.

TAKE GOD SERIOUSLY OR DON'T TAKE HIM AT ALL: LUKEWARMNESS KILLS

Rating:　　1　2　3　4　5　　　　Date Used:

460.   **IT'S WHO YOU KNOW
THAT DETERMINES
WHERE YOU GO
KNOW JESUS!**

Rating: 1   2   3   4   5   Date Used:

461.   **COOPERATION IS
SPELLED WITH
TWO LETTERS
—WE**

Rating: 1   2   3   4   5   Date Used:

462.   **FAILURE IS SUCCESS
IF WE LEARN
FROM IT**

Rating: 1   2   3   4   5   Date Used:

463.   **PEOPLE CAN ALTER
THEIR LIVES BY
ALTERING THEIR
ATTITUDES**

Rating: 1   2   3   4   5   Date Used:

464.   **YOU CANNOT SHAKE
HANDS WITH A
CLENCHED FIST**

Rating: 1   2   3   4   5   Date Used:

465.   **WHEN YOU CEASE TO
CONTRIBUTE YOU
BEGIN TO DIE**

Rating: 1   2   3   4   5   Date Used:

466.

WE CANNOT
DIRECT THE WIND
BUT WE CAN
ADJUST THE SAILS

Rating: 1   2   3   4   5   Date Used:

467.

PARALYZE RESISTANCE
WITH PERSISTENCE

Rating: 1   2   3   4   5   Date Used:

468.

LIFE WITHOUT LOVE
IS LIKE A TREE
WITHOUT LEAF OR
FRUIT

Rating: 1   2   3   4   5   Date Used:

469.

THE SUREST WAY TO
GO BROKE IS TO
SIT AROUND WAITING
FOR A BREAK

Rating: 1   2   3   4   5   Date Used:

470.

CHOICE NOT CHANCE
DETERMINES OUR
DESTINY

Rating: 1   2   3   4   5   Date Used:

471.

THE SMALLEST
GOOD DEED IS
BETTER THAN THE
GRANDEST INTENTION

Rating: 1   2   3   4   5   Date Used:

472.   **REAL LEADERS ARE ORDINARY PEOPLE WITH EXTRAORDINARY DETERMINATION**

Rating: 1   2   3   4   5   Date Used:

473.   **PURPOSE IS WHAT GIVES LIFE MEANING**

Rating: 1   2   3   4   5   Date Used:

474.   **WHERE THERE IS LOVE THERE IS LIFE**

Rating: 1   2   3   4   5   Date Used:

475.   **NO PROBLEM CAN STAND THE ASSAULT OF SUSTAINED EFFORT AND PRAYER**

Rating: 1   2   3   4   5   Date Used:

476.   **SIN WILL TAKE YOU FARTHER THAN YOU EVER WANT TO GO**

Rating: 1   2   3   4   5   Date Used:

477.   **THE SECRET TO SUCCESS IN LIFE IS TO KNOW WHO THE REAL BOSS IS**

Rating: 1   2   3   4   5   Date Used:

478.

**ONLY THOSE WHO
DARE TO FAIL GREATLY
ACHIEVE GREATLY**

Rating: 1 2 3 4 5   Date Used:

479.

**MOST PEOPLE ARE AS
HAPPY AS THEY MAKE
UP THEIR MINDS TO BE
—A. LINCOLN**

Rating: 1 2 3 4 5   Date Used:

480.

**IMPOSSIBILITY:
A WORD FOUND ONLY
IN THE DICTIONARY
OF FOOLS—NAPOLEON**

Rating: 1 2 3 4 5   Date Used:

481.

**INGENUITY
PLUS WORK PLUS
COURAGE PLUS GOD
EQUAL MIRACLES**

Rating: 1 2 3 4 5   Date Used:

482.

**PLEASURE IN THE JOB
PUTS PERFECTION IN
THE WORK—ARISTOTLE**

Rating: 1 2 3 4 5   Date Used:

483.

**LIFE IS LIKE A
BICYCLE—YOU DON'T
FALL OFF UNLESS YOU
STOP PEDALING**

Rating: 1 2 3 4 5   Date Used:

484.

A SHIP IN A HARBOR
IS SAFE, BUT SHIPS
ARE MADE FOR
SAILING

Rating: 1   2   3   4   5   Date Used:

485.

THE JOURNEY OF A
THOUSAND MILES
STARTS WITH A
SINGLE STEP

Rating: 1   2   3   4   5   Date Used:

486.

WE CAN ONLY HELP
OTHERS TO BE GOOD
IF WE ARE GOOD
OURSELVES

Rating: 1   2   3   4   5   Date Used:

487.

OPPORTUNITY IS
OFTEN HIDDEN IN
HARD WORK

Rating: 1   2   3   4   5   Date Used:

488.

GOOD IS NOT
ENOUGH WHERE
BETTER IS EXPECTED

Rating: 1   2   3   4   5   Date Used:

489.

IF GOD LIVES IN
YOUR NEIGHBOR
CONFLICT IS NOT
POSSIBLE

Rating: 1   2   3   4   5   Date Used:

490.

THE COMMANDS OF GOD ARE HARD ONLY FOR THOSE WHO RESIST THEM

Rating: 1 2 3 4 5　　　Date Used:

491.

IT IS THE SELF-RIGHTEOUSNESS OF THE PIOUS THAT BREEDS ATHEISM

Rating: 1 2 3 4 5　　　Date Used:

492.

SANCTIFIED AFFLICTIONS ARE SPIRITUAL PROMOTIONS

Rating: 1 2 3 4 5　　　Date Used:

493.

IT IS EASIER TO GET OLDER THAN IT IS TO GET WISER

Rating: 1 2 3 4 5　　　Date Used:

494.

IF GOD GAVE YOU THE SAME PRIORITY YOU GIVE HIM WOULD YOU BE SAVED?

Rating: 1 2 3 4 5　　　Date Used:

495.

YES, I BELIEVE IN GOD! —CASSIE BERNALL COLUMBINE H.S.

Rating: 1 2 3 4 5　　　Date Used:

496.

LOVE THE TRUE GOD —IF NOT, LOVE OF A FALSE GOD IS CERTAIN

Rating: 1   2   3   4   5   Date Used:

497.

LEAN ON THE CREATOR OR THE CREATURE— ONE UPLIFTS, ONE LETS DOWN

Rating: 1   2   3   4   5   Date Used:

498.

GOD IS YOUR HEAVENLY FATHER DON'T LIVE LIKE AN ORPHAN!

Rating: 1   2   3   4   5   Date Used:

499.

SIN IS THE ONLY THING GOD ABHORS

Rating: 1   2   3   4   5   Date Used:

500.

A GOOD RULE IS TO TREAT JESUS CHRIST AS A PERSONAL FRIEND

Rating: 1   2   3   4   5   Date Used:

501.

GOD WILL HONOR A PARENT WHO TRAINS A CHILD TO HONOR HIM

Rating: 1   2   3   4   5   Date Used:

502.

**BORN ONCE
DIE TWICE
—BORN TWICE
DIE ONCE**

Rating: 1   2   3   4   5   Date Used:

503.

**SERVICE CAN NEVER
BECOME SLAVERY
TO ONE WHO LOVES**

Rating: 1   2   3   4   5   Date Used:

504.

**LOVE IS THE MEDICINE
FOR THE SICKNESS
OF MANKIND
—KARL MENNINGER**

Rating: 1   2   3   4   5   Date Used:

505.

**GOD IS THE SOURCE
OF ALL TRUE
LASTING LOVE**

Rating: 1   2   3   4   5   Date Used:

506.

**WHEN WE LOVE WE
GIVE UP THE
CENTER OF OURSELVES
—ROLLO MAY**

Rating: 1   2   3   4   5   Date Used:

507.

**GOD HAS A BIG
ERASER!**

Rating: 1   2   3   4   5   Date Used:

508.   **NO CHRISTIANS HAVE
EVER BEEN KNOWN
TO RECANT ON THEIR
DEATH BED**

Rating: 1   2   3   4   5   Date Used:

509.   **YOU CAN NEVER BE
AN EFFECTIVE LEADER
UNTIL YOU LEARN TO
BE A SERVANT**

Rating: 1   2   3   4   5   Date Used:

510.   **LOVE CURES PEOPLE—
BOTH THOSE WHO GIVE
IT AND THOSE WHO
RECEIVE IT**

Rating: 1   2   3   4   5   Date Used:

511.   **WHEN THINGS
GO WRONG
DON'T GO
WITH THEM**

Rating: 1   2   3   4   5   Date Used:

512.   **CHURCH IS A HOSPITAL
FOR SINNERS NOT
A MUSEUM FOR
SAINTS**

Rating: 1   2   3   4   5   Date Used:

513.   **SOME THINGS HAVE
TO BE BELIEVED TO
BE SEEN**

Rating: 1   2   3   4   5   Date Used:

514.   **LITTLE AND OFTEN
MAKE MUCH**

Rating: 1   2   3   4   5   Date Used:

515.   **THIS CHURCH IS A
CERTIFIED BURDEN
DROP-OFF CENTER**

Rating: 1   2   3   4   5   Date Used:

516.   **GOD ALREADY MADE
MY DAY!**

Rating: 1   2   3   4   5   Date Used:

517.   **HE THAT FEEDS THE
BIRDS WILL NOT
STARVE HIS CHILDREN**

Rating: 1   2   3   4   5   Date Used:

518.   **A TRYING TIME IS
NO TIME TO QUIT
TRYING**

Rating: 1   2   3   4   5   Date Used:

519.   **ONLY GOD IS IN A
POSITION TO LOOK
DOWN ON ANYONE**

Rating: 1   2   3   4   5   Date Used:

520.   **PRAYING HANDS
CAN'T BE PREYING
HANDS**

Rating: 1   2   3   4   5   Date Used:

521. **CARRY A GRUDGE
AND IT GETS HEAVIER
WITH EACH STEP**

Rating: 1 2 3 4 5 Date Used:

522. **GOD HAS PLANTED US
A GARDEN BUT WE
MUST KEEP IT WEEDED**

Rating: 1 2 3 4 5 Date Used:

523. **GOD MADE TWO EARS
THAT STAY OPEN
AND ONE MOUTH
THAT CAN BE SHUT**

Rating: 1 2 3 4 5 Date Used:

524. **IT IS BETTER TO DIE
WELL THAN TO LIVE ILL**

Rating: 1 2 3 4 5 Date Used:

525. **FORCE IS WEAKNESS
LOVE IS POWER**

Rating: 1 2 3 4 5 Date Used:

526. **THERE IS NO LIMIT TO
THE GOOD WE CAN DO
IF WE DON'T NEED TO
HAVE CREDIT**

Rating: 1 2 3 4 5 Date Used:

527. **LOVE IS GOD
WITHIN YOU**

Rating: 1 2 3 4 5 Date Used:

528.
LIVE FOR THIS LIFE ALONE AND YOU WILL MISS THE NEXT ONE

Rating: 1   2   3   4   5   Date Used:

529.
WORK FOR THE LORD —THE RETIREMENT BENEFITS ARE OUT OF THIS WORLD

Rating: 1   2   3   4   5   Date Used:

530.
LIVE LIFE AS IF THIS IS ALL THERE IS AND IT WILL BE

Rating: 1   2   3   4   5   Date Used:

531.
THE NEXT LIFE IS MORE IMPORTANT THAN THIS ONE

Rating: 1   2   3   4   5   Date Used:

532.
LIVE FOR TODAY ONLY AND YOU'LL MISS A FANTASTIC TOMORROW

Rating: 1   2   3   4   5   Date Used:

533.
GOD WANTS US TO READ PSALMS NOT PALMS

Rating: 1   2   3   4   5   Date Used:

534.   **LITTLE IS MUCH IN THE HANDS OF JESUS**

Rating: 1   2   3   4   5   Date Used:

535.   **DOUBTS AND FEARS CRUMBLE UNDER THE WEIGHT OF GOD'S PROMISES**

Rating: 1   2   3   4   5   Date Used:

536.   **GOD ALMIGHTY LIVING WITHIN US— THAT'S WHAT ETERNAL LIFE IS**

Rating: 1   2   3   4   5   Date Used:

537.   **BY TRIALS GOD IS SHAPING US FOR HIGHER THINGS**

Rating: 1   2   3   4   5   Date Used:

538.   **ROCK BOTTOM ISN'T BAD IF YOU ARE STANDING ON THE SOLID ROCK OF JESUS**

Rating: 1   2   3   4   5   Date Used:

539.   **THERE IS WONDER-WORKING POWER IN THE BLOOD OF JESUS**

Rating: 1   2   3   4   5   Date Used:

540. **IF YOU ACCEPT GOD'S SON HE ACCEPTS YOU**

Rating: 1   2   3   4   5   Date Used:

541. **NO ONE KNOWS HOW BAD THEY ARE UNTIL THEY TRY TO BE GOOD**

Rating: 1   2   3   4   5   Date Used:

542. **TO MASTER TEMPTATION YOU MUST FIRST LET CHRIST MASTER YOU**

Rating: 1   2   3   4   5   Date Used:

543. **THE VOICE OF SIN IS LOUD BUT THE VOICE OF FORGIVENESS IS LOUDER—D. L. MOODY**

Rating: 1   2   3   4   5   Date Used:

544. **CHRIST BRINGS AN INNER PEACE THAT PASSES ALL UNDERSTANDING**

Rating: 1   2   3   4   5   Date Used:

545. **THE WAY TO HEAVEN IS DOWNHILL NOT UPHILL—HIS YOKE IS EASY**

Rating: 1   2   3   4   5   Date Used:

546.   THE GOOD NEWS IS
                   THE BAD NEWS
                      IS WRONG

Rating: 1   2   3   4   5   Date Used:

547.   IN THE BEGINNING
                  GOD CREATED THE
                    HEAVEN AND
                  EARTH—GEN. 1:1

Rating: 1   2   3   4   5   Date Used:

548.   REMEMBER THE
                  SABBATH DAY TO
                   KEEP IT HOLY
                   —EXOD. 20:8

Rating: 1   2   3   4   5   Date Used:

549.   DO NOT FOLLOW
                    THE CROWD
                  IN DOING WRONG
                   —EXOD. 23:2

Rating: 1   2   3   4   5   Date Used:

550.   BLESSED BE THE NAME
                    OF THE LORD
                     —JOB 1:21

Rating: 1   2   3   4   5   Date Used:

551.   THOUGH HE SLAY ME
                  YET WILL I TRUST
                        HIM
                    —JOB 13:15

Rating: 1   2   3   4   5   Date Used:

552.

WHEN HE TRIED ME
I CAME FORTH AS
GOLD
—JOB 23:10

Rating: 1 2 3 4 5   Date Used:

553.

THE FOOL SAYS IN
HIS HEART THERE
IS NO GOD
—PS. 14:1

Rating: 1 2 3 4 5   Date Used:

554.

THE SORROWS OF THOSE
WILL INCREASE WHO
RUN AFTER OTHER
GODS—PS. 16:4

Rating: 1 2 3 4 5   Date Used:

555.

MY GOD
TURNS MY DARKNESS
INTO LIGHT
—PS. 18:28

Rating: 1 2 3 4 5   Date Used:

556.

HE IS A SHIELD
FOR ALL WHO
TAKE REFUGE IN HIM
—PS. 18:30

Rating: 1 2 3 4 5   Date Used:

557.

YOU GIVE ME YOUR
SHIELD OF VICTORY
AND YOUR RIGHT HAND
SUSTAINS ME—PS. 18:35

Rating: 1 2 3 4 5   Date Used:

558.   **HE RESTORES MY
SOUL
—PS. 23:3**

Rating: 1   2   3   4   5   Date Used:

559.   **WAIT FOR THE LORD
BE STRONG
AND TAKE HEART
—PS. 27:14**

Rating: 1   2   3   4   5   Date Used:

560.   **THE LORD BLESSES HIS
PEOPLE WITH PEACE
—PS. 29:11**

Rating: 1   2   3   4   5   Date Used:

561.   **WEEPING MAY ENDURE
FOR A NIGHT BUT JOY
COMES IN THE
MORNING—PS. 30:5**

Rating: 1   2   3   4   5   Date Used:

562.   **O TASTE AND SEE
THE LORD IS GOOD
—PS. 34:8**

Rating: 1   2   3   4   5   Date Used:

563.   **THE LORD SAVES
THOSE WHO ARE
CRUSHED IN SPIRIT
—PS. 34:18**

Rating: 1   2   3   4   5   Date Used:

564.

THE WICKED BORROW AND DO NOT REPAY BUT THE RIGHTEOUS GIVE GENEROUSLY—PS. 37:21

Rating: 1 2 3 4 5   Date Used:

565.

I WAITED PATIENTLY FOR THE LORD AND HE TURNED TO ME AND HEARD MY CRY—PS. 40:1

Rating: 1 2 3 4 5   Date Used:

566.

CAST YOUR BURDEN ON THE LORD AND HE WILL SUSTAIN YOU —PS. 55:22

Rating: 1 2 3 4 5   Date Used:

567.

NO GOOD THING DOES HE WITHHOLD FROM THOSE THAT WALK UPRIGHTLY—PS. 84:11

Rating: 1 2 3 4 5   Date Used:

568.

BLESS THE LORD O MY SOUL . . . BLESS HIS HOLY NAME —PS. 103:1

Rating: 1 2 3 4 5   Date Used:

569.

THE LORD PITIES THOSE WHO FEAR HIM —PS. 103:13

Rating: 1 2 3 4 5   Date Used:

570.   **THY WORD HAVE I
                      HID IN MY HEART
                      —PS. 119:11**

Rating: 1   2   3   4   5   Date Used:

571.   **YOUR WORD IS A LAMP
                      TO MY FEET AND A
                      LIGHT FOR MY PATH
                      —PS. 119:105**

Rating: 1   2   3   4   5   Date Used:

572.   **I CALL ON THE LORD
                      IN MY DISTRESS AND
                      HE ANSWERS ME
                      —PS. 120:1**

Rating: 1   2   3   4   5   Date Used:

573.   **HE WILL NOT LET
                      YOUR FOOT SLIP
                      —PS. 121:3**

Rating: 1   2   3   4   5   Date Used:

574.   **THOSE WHO SOW
                      IN TEARS SHALL
                      REAP IN JOY
                      —PS. 126:5**

Rating: 1   2   3   4   5   Date Used:

575.   **PUT YOUR HOPE
                      IN THE LORD BOTH
                      NOW AND EVERMORE
                      —PS. 131:3**

Rating: 1   2   3   4   5   Date Used:

576.   **HIS MERCY ENDURES**
                  FOREVER
                  —PS. 136:1

Rating: 1   2   3   4   5   Date Used:

577.   **THE LORD IS GRACIOUS**
                  AND COMPASSIONATE
                  SLOW TO ANGER AND
                  RICH IN LOVE—PS. 145:8

Rating: 1   2   3   4   5   Date Used:

578.   **GREAT IS OUR LORD**
                  AND MIGHTY IN
                  POWER
                  —PS. 147:5

Rating: 1   2   3   4   5   Date Used:

579.   **LET THE WISE LISTEN**
                  AND ADD TO THEIR
                  LEARNING
                  —PROV. 1:5

Rating: 1   2   3   4   5   Date Used:

580.   **LISTEN MY SON TO**
                  YOUR FATHER'S
                  INSTRUCTION
                  —PROV. 1:8

Rating: 1   2   3   4   5   Date Used:

581.   **DO NOT BE WISE IN**
                  YOUR OWN EYES
                  —PROV. 3:7

Rating: 1   2   3   4   5   Date Used:

582.

HONOR THE LORD
WITH YOUR WEALTH
—PROV. 3:9

Rating: 1 2 3 4 5 Date Used:

583.

MY SON DO NOT
DESPISE THE LORD'S
DISCIPLINE
—PROV. 3:11

Rating: 1 2 3 4 5 Date Used:

584.

WISDOM IS SUPREME
THEREFORE GET
WISDOM
—PROV. 4:7

Rating: 1 2 3 4 5 Date Used:

585.

A MAN'S WAYS ARE
IN FULL VIEW OF
THE LORD
—PROV. 5:21

Rating: 1 2 3 4 5 Date Used:

586.

THE PROSPECT OF
THE RIGHTEOUS IS JOY
—PROV. 10:28

Rating: 1 2 3 4 5 Date Used:

587.

WHOEVER TRUSTS IN
HIS RICHES WILL FALL
—PROV. 11:28

Rating: 1 2 3 4 5 Date Used:

588.

**HE WHO FEARS THE
LORD HAS A SECURE
FORTRESS
—PROV. 14:26**

Rating: 1   2   3   4   5   Date Used:

589.

**THE FEAR OF THE
LORD IS A FOUNTAIN
OF LIFE
—PROV. 14:27**

Rating: 1   2   3   4   5   Date Used:

590.

**RIGHTEOUSNESS EXALTS
A NATION, BUT SIN IS A
DISGRACE TO ANY
PEOPLE—PROV. 14:34**

Rating: 1   2   3   4   5   Date Used:

591.

**A SOFT ANSWER
TURNS AWAY WRATH
—PROV. 15:1**

Rating: 1   2   3   4   5   Date Used:

592.

**A HAPPY HEART
MAKES THE FACE
CHEERFUL
—PROV. 15:13**

Rating: 1   2   3   4   5   Date Used:

593.

**A GREEDY MAN
BRINGS TROUBLE
TO HIS FAMILY
—PROV. 15:27**

Rating: 1   2   3   4   5   Date Used:

594.

THE HEART OF THE RIGHTEOUS WEIGHS ITS ANSWERS
—PROV. 15:28

Rating: 1   2   3   4   5   Date Used:

595.

PLEASANT WORDS ARE A HEALING TO THE BONES
—PROV. 16:24

Rating: 1   2   3   4   5   Date Used:

596.

A CHEERFUL HEART IS GOOD MEDICINE
—PROV. 17:22

Rating: 1   2   3   4   5   Date Used:

597.

THERE IS A FRIEND WHO STICKS CLOSER THAN A BROTHER
—PROV. 18:24

Rating: 1   2   3   4   5   Date Used:

598.

DO NOT WEAR OUT YOURSELF TO GET RICH
—PROV. 23:4

Rating: 1   2   3   4   5   Date Used:

599.

MY SON GIVE ME YOUR HEART AND LET YOUR EYES KEEP TO MY WAY
—PROV. 23:26

Rating: 1   2   3   4   5   Date Used:

600.

AN HONEST ANSWER
IS LIKE A KISS ON
THE LIPS
—PROV. 24:26

Rating: 1   2   3   4   5   Date Used:

601.

A MAN'S PRIDE
BRINGS HIM LOW
—PROV. 29:23

Rating: 1   2   3   4   5   Date Used:

602.

EVERY WORD OF GOD
IS FLAWLESS
—PROV. 30:5

Rating: 1   2   3   4   5   Date Used:

603.

WHATEVER YOUR HAND
FINDS TO DO, DO IT
WITH ALL YOUR MIGHT
—ECCL. 9:10

Rating: 1   2   3   4   5   Date Used:

604.

IN QUIETNESS
AND TRUST
IS YOUR STRENGTH
—ISA. 30:15

Rating: 1   2   3   4   5   Date Used:

605.

THOSE WHO HOPE IN
THE LORD WILL RENEW
THEIR STRENGTH
—ISA. 40:31

Rating: 1   2   3   4   5   Date Used:

606.   **BEHOLD, I HAVE
ENGRAVED YOU ON
THE PALM OF MY HAND
—ISA. 49:16**

Rating: 1   2   3   4   5   Date Used:

607.   **BY HIS STRIPES
WE ARE HEALED
—ISA. 53:5**

Rating: 1   2   3   4   5   Date Used:

608.   **LET THE WICKED
FORSAKE HIS WAY
—ISA. 55:7**

Rating: 1   2   3   4   5   Date Used:

609.   **HE WILL ABUNDANTLY
PARDON
—ISA. 55:7**

Rating: 1   2   3   4   5   Date Used:

610.   **I HAVE LOVED YOU
WITH AN EVERLASTING
LOVE
—JER. 31:3**

Rating: 1   2   3   4   5   Date Used:

611.   **PREPARE TO MEET
YOUR GOD
—AMOS 4:12**

Rating: 1   2   3   4   5   Date Used:

612.

THE JUST SHALL LIVE BY HIS FAITH
—HAB. 2:4

Rating: 1   2   3   4   5   Date Used:

613.

AND THEY SHALL CALL HIS NAME IMMANUEL MEANING GOD WITH US
—MATT. 1:23

Rating: 1   2   3   4   5   Date Used:

614.

BLESSED ARE THE MERCIFUL FOR THEY WILL BE SHOWN MERCY—MATT. 5:7

Rating: 1   2   3   4   5   Date Used:

615.

WHEN YOU PRAY ENTER INTO YOUR CLOSET
—MATT. 6:6

Rating: 1   2   3   4   5   Date Used:

616.

IF YOU FORGIVE MEN YOUR HEAVENLY FATHER WILL FORGIVE YOU
—MATT. 6:14

Rating: 1   2   3   4   5   Date Used:

617.

LAY NOT UP FOR YOURSELVES TREASURES ON EARTH
—MATT. 6:19

Rating: 1   2   3   4   5   Date Used:

618.   **WHERE YOUR
                    TREASURE IS, THERE
                    YOUR HEART WILL
                    BE ALSO—MATT. 6:21**

Rating: 1   2   3   4   5   Date Used:

619.   **YOU CANNOT SERVE
                    BOTH GOD AND
                    MONEY
                    —MATT. 6:24**

Rating: 1   2   3   4   5   Date Used:

620.   **SEEK YE FIRST THE
                    KINGDOM OF GOD
                    —MATT. 6:33**

Rating: 1   2   3   4   5   Date Used:

621.   **BROAD IS THE ROAD
                    THAT LEADS TO
                    DESTRUCTION
                    —MATT. 7:13**

Rating: 1   2   3   4   5   Date Used:

622.   **FOR MY YOKE IS EASY
                    —MATT. 11:30**

Rating: 1   2   3   4   5   Date Used:

623.   **HE WHO IS NOT
                    WITH ME IS
                    AGAINST ME—JESUS
                    —MATT. 12:30**

Rating: 1   2   3   4   5   Date Used:

624.

THE SON OF MAN WILL COME AT AN HOUR WHEN YOU DO NOT EXPECT HIM—MATT. 24:44

Rating: 1   2   3   4   5   Date Used:

625.

LORD I BELIEVE HELP THOU MY UNBELIEF —MARK 9:24

Rating: 1   2   3   4   5   Date Used:

626.

WHOEVER BELIEVES WILL BE SAVED —MARK 16:16

Rating: 1   2   3   4   5   Date Used:

627.

WHEN YOU PRAY, SAY FATHER . . . —LUKE 11:2

Rating: 1   2   3   4   5   Date Used:

628.

BEHOLD, THE LAMB OF GOD WHO TAKES AWAY THE SINS OF THE WORLD—JOHN 1:29

Rating: 1   2   3   4   5   Date Used:

629.

HIM THAT COMETH TO ME I WILL IN NO WISE CAST OUT —JOHN 6:37

Rating: 1   2   3   4   5   Date Used:

630.

HE THAT BELIEVES ON ME HAS EVERLASTING LIFE
—JOHN 6:47

Rating: 1 2 3 4 5   Date Used:

631.

THE TRUTH WILL SET YOU FREE
—JOHN 8:32

Rating: 1 2 3 4 5   Date Used:

632.

I AM COME THAT THEY MIGHT HAVE LIFE MORE ABUNDANTLY
—JOHN 10:10

Rating: 1 2 3 4 5   Date Used:

633.

MY SHEEP LISTEN TO MY VOICE; I KNOW THEM AND THEY FOLLOW ME—JOHN 10:27

Rating: 1 2 3 4 5   Date Used:

634.

DO NOT LET YOUR HEARTS BE TROUBLED TRUST IN GOD
—JOHN 14:1

Rating: 1 2 3 4 5   Date Used:

635.

NO ONE COMES TO THE FATHER EXCEPT THROUGH ME—JESUS
—JOHN 14:6

Rating: 1 2 3 4 5   Date Used:

636.

**IF YOU LOVE ME YOU
WILL KEEP MY
COMMANDMENTS
—JOHN 14:15**

Rating: 1   2   3   4   5   Date Used:

637.

**BECAUSE I LIVE YOU
SHALL LIVE ALSO
—JOHN 14:19**

Rating: 1   2   3   4   5   Date Used:

638.

**EVERY BRANCH THAT
BEARS FRUIT HE
PURGES
—JOHN 15:2**

Rating: 1   2   3   4   5   Date Used:

639.

**THIS IS MY COMMAND:
LOVE EACH OTHER!
—JESUS
—JOHN 15:17**

Rating: 1   2   3   4   5   Date Used:

640.

**YOUR SORROW WILL
BE TURNED INTO JOY
—JOHN 16:20**

Rating: 1   2   3   4   5   Date Used:

641.

**IN THIS WORLD
YOU WILL HAVE
TROUBLE
—JOHN 16:33**

Rating: 1   2   3   4   5   Date Used:

642.
TAKE COURAGE FOR I HAVE OVERCOME THE WORLD—JESUS —JOHN 16:33

Rating: 1 2 3 4 5 Date Used:

643.
BY THE LAW IS THE KNOWLEDGE OF SIN —ROM. 3:20

Rating: 1 2 3 4 5 Date Used:

644.
FOR ALL HAVE SINNED AND FALL SHORT OF THE GLORY OF GOD —ROM. 3:23

Rating: 1 2 3 4 5 Date Used:

645.
GOD HAS POURED OUT HIS LOVE INTO OUR HEARTS BY THE HOLY SPIRIT—ROM. 5:5

Rating: 1 2 3 4 5 Date Used:

646.
CHRIST DIED FOR THE UNGODLY —ROM. 5:6

Rating: 1 2 3 4 5 Date Used:

647.
THE WAGES OF SIN IS DEATH, THE GIFT OF GOD IS ETERNAL LIFE—ROM. 6:23

Rating: 1 2 3 4 5 Date Used:

648.

**THERE IS NOW NO
CONDEMNATION TO
THOSE WHO ARE IN
CHRIST JESUS—ROM. 8:1**

Rating: 1 2 3 4 5 Date Used:

649.

**THE SINFUL MIND
IS HOSTILE TO GOD
—ROM. 8:7**

Rating: 1 2 3 4 5 Date Used:

650.

**IF YOU LIVE ACCORDING
TO THE FLESH YOU
WILL DIE
—ROM. 8:13**

Rating: 1 2 3 4 5 Date Used:

651.

**IF GOD IS FOR US,
WHO CAN BE
AGAINST US?
—ROM. 8:31**

Rating: 1 2 3 4 5 Date Used:

652.

**WHO WILL SEPARATE
US FROM THE LOVE OF
CHRIST?
—ROM. 8:35**

Rating: 1 2 3 4 5 Date Used:

653.

**EVERYONE WHO
CALLS ON THE NAME OF
THE LORD WILL BE
SAVED—ROM. 10:13**

Rating: 1 2 3 4 5 Date Used:

654.   **DO NOT CONFORM
TO THIS WORLD . . .
BE TRANSFORMED
—ROM. 12:2**

Rating: 1   2   3   4   5   Date Used:

655.   **HATE WHAT IS EVIL
CLING TO WHAT
IS GOOD
—ROM. 12:9**

Rating: 1   2   3   4   5   Date Used:

656.   **BE JOYFUL IN HOPE,
PATIENT IN
AFFLICTION, FAITHFUL
IN PRAYER—ROM. 12:12**

Rating: 1   2   3   4   5   Date Used:

657.   **DO NOT REPAY
ANYONE EVIL FOR
EVIL
—ROM. 12:17**

Rating: 1   2   3   4   5   Date Used:

658.   **IF IT IS POSSIBLE
LIVE AT PEACE WITH
EVERYONE
—ROM. 12:18**

Rating: 1   2   3   4   5   Date Used:

659.   **DO NOT TAKE REVENGE
LEAVE ROOM FOR
GOD'S WRATH
—ROM. 12:19**

Rating: 1   2   3   4   5   Date Used:

660.

YOU WERE BOUGHT
AT A PRICE . . . HONOR
GOD WITH YOUR BODY
—1 COR. 6:20

Rating: 1   2   3   4   5   Date Used:

661.

THE LAST ENEMY
TO BE DESTROYED
IS DEATH
—1 COR. 15:26

Rating: 1   2   3   4   5   Date Used:

662.

STAND FIRM . . . YOUR
LABOR IN THE LORD
IS NOT IN VAIN
—1 COR. 15:58

Rating: 1   2   3   4   5   Date Used:

663.

DO NOT BE YOKED
TOGETHER WITH
UNBELIEVERS
—2 COR. 6:14

Rating: 1   2   3   4   5   Date Used:

664.

THANKS BE TO
GOD FOR HIS
INDESCRIBABLE
GIFT—2 COR. 9:15

Rating: 1   2   3   4   5   Date Used:

665.

CARRY EACH OTHER'S
BURDENS . . . YOU WILL
FULFILL THE LAW OF
CHRIST—GAL. 6:2

Rating: 1   2   3   4   5   Date Used:

666.

THE ONLY THING THAT COUNTS IS FAITH EXPRESSING ITSELF THROUGH LOVE—GAL. 4:6

Rating: 1   2   3   4   5   Date Used:

667.

BY GRACE ARE YE SAVED AND THAT NOT OF YOURSELVES IT IS THE GIFT OF GOD—EPH. 2:8

Rating: 1   2   3   4   5   Date Used:

668.

BE KIND AND COMPASSIONATE TO ONE ANOTHER —EPH. 4:32

Rating: 1   2   3   4   5   Date Used:

669.

BE CAREFUL HOW YOU LIVE BECAUSE THE DAYS ARE EVIL —EPH. 5:15–16

Rating: 1   2   3   4   5   Date Used:

670.

PUT ON THE FULL ARMOR OF GOD —EPH. 6:11

Rating: 1   2   3   4   5   Date Used:

671.

FOR ME TO LIVE IS CHRIST AND TO DIE IS GAIN—ST. PAUL —PHIL. 1:21

Rating: 1   2   3   4   5   Date Used:

672.

**DO EVERYTHING
WITHOUT COMPLAINING
OR ARGUING
—PHIL. 2:14**

Rating: 1 2 3 4 5   Date Used:

673.

**BE ANXIOUS FOR
NOTHING
—PHIL. 4:6**

Rating: 1 2 3 4 5   Date Used:

674.

**I HAVE LEARNED TO BE
CONTENT WHATEVER
THE CIRCUMSTANCE
—PHIL. 4:11**

Rating: 1 2 3 4 5   Date Used:

675.

**I CAN DO EVERYTHING
THROUGH CHRIST WHO
STRENGTHENS ME
—PHIL. 4:13**

Rating: 1 2 3 4 5   Date Used:

676.

**ENCOURAGE ONE
ANOTHER AND BUILD
EACH OTHER UP
—1 THESS. 5:11**

Rating: 1 2 3 4 5   Date Used:

677.

**PRAY WITHOUT
CEASING
—1 THESS. 5:17**

Rating: 1 2 3 4 5   Date Used:

678.
THE ONE WHO CALLS YOU
IS FAITHFUL
—1 THESS. 5:24

Rating: 1 2 3 4 5   Date Used:

679.
NEVER TIRE OF DOING
WHAT IS RIGHT
—2 THESS. 3:13

Rating: 1 2 3 4 5   Date Used:

680.
THERE IS ONE
MEDIATOR BETWEEN
GOD AND MAN. . . CHRIST
JESUS—1 TIM. 2:5

Rating: 1 2 3 4 5   Date Used:

681.
TRAIN YOURSELF
TO BE GODLY
—1 TIM. 4:7

Rating: 1 2 3 4 5   Date Used:

682.
PEOPLE WHO WANT
TO GET RICH FALL
INTO TEMPTATION
—1 TIM. 6:9

Rating: 1 2 3 4 5   Date Used:

683.
THE LOVE OF MONEY
IS A ROOT OF ALL
KINDS OF EVIL
—1 TIM. 6:10

Rating: 1 2 3 4 5   Date Used:

684.

**ALL SCRIPTURE IS
GIVEN BY THE
INSPIRATION OF GOD
—2 TIM. 3:16**

Rating: 1   2   3   4   5   Date Used:

685.

**CORRECT, REBUKE, AND
ENCOURAGE WITH GREAT
PATIENCE AND CAREFUL
INSTRUCTION—2 TIM. 4:2**

Rating: 1   2   3   4   5   Date Used:

686.

**THE WORD OF GOD IS
SHARPER THAN ANY
TWO-EDGED SWORD
—HEB. 4:12**

Rating: 1   2   3   4   5   Date Used:

687.

**KEEP YOUR LIVES
FREE FROM THE LOVE
OF MONEY
—HEB. 13:5**

Rating: 1   2   3   4   5   Date Used:

688.

**GOD HAS SAID: NEVER
WILL I LEAVE YOU
NEVER WILL I FORSAKE
YOU—HEB. 13:5**

Rating: 1   2   3   4   5   Date Used:

689.

**EVERYONE SHOULD BE
QUICK TO LISTEN SLOW
TO SPEAK AND SLOW TO
BECOME ANGRY—JAMES 1:19**

Rating: 1   2   3   4   5   Date Used:

690.

**DO NOT MERELY
LISTEN TO THE WORD
. . . DO WHAT IT SAYS
—JAMES 1:22**

Rating: 1 2 3 4 5 Date Used:

691.

**KNOW YE NOT THAT
FRIENDSHIP WITH THE
WORLD IS ENMITY WITH
GOD!—JAMES 4:4**

Rating: 1 2 3 4 5 Date Used:

692.

**HUMBLE YOURSELVES
BEFORE THE LORD AND
HE WILL LIFT YOU UP
—JAMES 4:10**

Rating: 1 2 3 4 5 Date Used:

693.

**THE PRAYER OF FAITH
SHALL SAVE THE SICK
—JAMES 5:15**

Rating: 1 2 3 4 5 Date Used:

694.

**THE PRAYER OF A
RIGHTEOUS MAN
IS POWERFUL AND
EFFECTIVE—JAMES 5:16**

Rating: 1 2 3 4 5 Date Used:

695.

**LOVE EACH OTHER
BECAUSE LOVE COVERS
A MULTITUDE OF SINS
—1 PETER 4:8**

Rating: 1 2 3 4 5 Date Used:

696.

CAST ALL YOUR CARE UPON HIM FOR HE CARES FOR YOU —1 PETER 5:7

Rating: 1   2   3   4   5   Date Used:

697.

THE LORD IS NOT WILLING THAT ANY SHOULD PERISH —2 PETER 3:9

Rating: 1   2   3   4   5   Date Used:

698.

IF WE CONFESS OUR SINS HE IS FAITHFUL TO FORGIVE US —1 JOHN 1:9

Rating: 1   2   3   4   5   Date Used:

699.

BE FAITHFUL UNTO DEATH AND I WILL GIVE YOU A CROWN OF LIFE—REV. 2:10

Rating: 1   2   3   4   5   Date Used:

700.

BECAUSE YOU ARE LUKEWARM I WILL SPEW YOU OUT OF MY MOUTH—REV. 3:16

Rating: 1   2   3   4   5   Date Used:

701.

GOD SHALL WIPE AWAY ALL TEARS FROM THEIR EYES —REV. 21:4

Rating: 1   2   3   4   5   Date Used:

A second volume of *Sentence Sermons* is being developed by Dr. Harvey. You are invited to participate. Included in the second book will be a number of stories like the one about Cassie Bernall found in the introduction to this volume. These will be stories that tell of the impact of sentence sermons on people's lives. If you have a sentence sermon or a story you would like to submit for possible publication, please mail it to:

> Dr. L. James Harvey
> 12400 Appleby Ct.
> Upper Marlboro, MD 20772
>
> or send by fax to: (301) 627-5976
> or by e-mail to: jharvey@olg.com

All submissions are subject to editing and cannot be returned. You will be notified if your item is accepted, and your name will be acknowledged in the book. All rights to submitted material will be retained by the author. Those who have stories published will receive a complimentary copy of the book in lieu of payment.

Sentence Sermon Topics and Sources

(listed by sermon number)

A

Abortion, 64, 67
Achievement, 303, 420
Adversity, 246
Advice, 77
Afflictions, 492
Aging, 218, 290, 291
America, 60
Angels, 155
Anger, 152, 355, 464, 689 (James 1:19)
Anxiety, 165, 673 (Phil. 4:6)
Apathy, 324
Arguments, 49
Aristotle, 482
Armor, 670 (Eph. 6:11)
Atheism, 78, 84, 306, 359, 491, 553 (Ps. 14:1)
Attitude, 416, 463, 466, 519
Availability, 415

B

Bacon, Francis, 177
Baptism, 294
Beauty, 151
Belief, 50, 92, 495, 513, 625 (Mark 9:24), 626 (Mark 16:16), 630 (John 6:47)
Bernall, Cassie, 495
Bible, 43, 106, 111, 140, 144, 208, 325, 336, 441, 533, 570 (Ps. 119:11), 571 (Ps. 119:105), 684 (2 Tim. 3:16)
Browning, Robert, 80
Budget, 72
Burden, 566 (Ps. 55:22), 665 (Gal. 6:2)
Burns, Robert, 176
Busyness, 122

C

Calvin, John, 156
Careers, 235
Caring, 696 (1 Peter 5:7)
Change, 26, 285, 448
Channing, Wm. E., 91
Character, 30, 91, 151
Cheerfulness, 596 (Prov. 17:22)
Chesterton, G. K., 124, 155
Children, 9, 51, 54, 65, 67
Choice, 470
Christ, 164, 187, 188, 189, 245, 646 (Rom. 5:16), 648 (Rom. 8:1), 680 (1 Tim. 2:5)
Christianity, 16, 300, 334, 374, 427
Christmas, 57, 58, 304
Church, 31, 104, 116, 167, 168, 172, 453, 454, 512, 515
Churchill, Winston, 25, 90
Circumstances, 109, 267
Coffee hour, 126
Companionship, 96
Confession, 6
Conflict, 489
Conscience, 58, 93, 320, 392
Contentment, 88, 215, 396, 397, 674 (Phil. 4:11)
Conviction, 362, 373, 541
Cooperation, 391, 461
Correction, 685 (2 Tim. 4:2)
Courage, 385, 484, 485
Creation, 11, 82, 547 (Gen. 1:1)
Cross, 24, 71, 136, 227, 363
Cynic, 105

D

Death, 147, 166, 255, 465, 661 (1 Cor. 15:26)
Debt, 422
Deeds, 346, 471
Despair, 100, 247, 445
Destruction, 621 (Matt. 7:13)

Devil, 312, 368
Difficulties, 5, 90, 193
Discipline, 369, 583 (Prov. 3:11)
Distress, 23, 343
Doubt, 358, 401
Drunkenness, 150

E

Easter, 59, 138, 161
Effectiveness, 204
Egotists, 119, 125
Encouragement, 185, 209, 339, 531, 532, 676 (1 Thess. 5:11)
Energy, 190
Enmity, 691 (James 4:4)
Error, 128
Eternity, 183, 229, 249, 269, 365, 455
Ethics, 7, 389, 407, 408, 511, 679 (2 Thess. 3:13)
Evangelism, 31
Evil, 157, 437, 657 (Rom. 12:17)
Excellence, 134, 488, 603 (Eccl. 9:10)
Experience, 52
Expenses, 95

F

Failure, 37, 130, 170, 201, 222, 299, 388, 462, 478
Faith, 10, 11, 34, 98, 124, 244, 270, 295, 370, 382, 398, 399, 411, 431, 432, 452, 612 (Hab. 2:4), 666 (Gal. 4:6)
Faithfulness, 142, 678 (1 Thess. 5:24), 699 (Rev. 2:10)
Family, 97
Father, 498
Fear, 213, 366, 428, 569 (Ps. 103:13), 588 (Prov. 14:26), 589 (Prov. 14:27)
Flesh, 650 (Rom. 8:13)
Fool, 99

Forgiveness, 63, 121, 145, 192, 261, 349, 418, 425, 457, 507, 543, 616 (Matt. 6:14), 698 (1 John 1:9)
Franklin, Ben, 58, 95
Friendship, 139, 383, 436, 597 (Prov. 18:24)
Fun, 27, 124

G
Gambling, 12, 273
Gentleness, 352
Giving, 1, 41, 117, 214, 219, 292, 316, 318, 319, 340, 371, 423, 564 (Ps. 37:21)
God, 2, 21, 36, 42, 70, 82, 110, 186, 211, 225, 257, 258, 297, 298, 323, 327, 335, 341, 497, 516, 517, 651 (Rom. 8:31)
Godliness, 681 (1 Tim. 4:7)
Good news, 546
Good works, 120
Goodness, 486, 526, 655 (Rom. 12:9)
Gospels, 372
Gossip, 197
Grace, 191, 194, 417, 667 (Eph. 2:8)
Grant, U. S., 322
Greed, 117, 158, 593 (Prov. 15:27)
Grudge, 521

H
Happiness, 13, 25, 479, 592 (Prov. 15:13)
Health, 287
Heaven, 39, 254, 311, 442, 545
Hell, 45, 81
Holy Spirit, 645 (Rom. 5:5)
Home, 350
Honesty, 176, 410, 600 (Prov. 24:26)

Honor, 163, 582 (Prov. 3:9), 602, 660 (1 Cor. 6:20)
Hope, 38, 212, 575 (Ps. 131:3)
Hospitality, 131
Humility, 14, 62, 115, 226, 692 (James 4:10)
Humor, 403
Hypocrisy, 374

I
Immanuel, 613 (Matt. 1:23)
Immaturity, 148
Impossibility, 480
Improvement, 123
Instruction, 580 (Prov. 1:8)
Investments, 76

J
Jackson, Andrew, 325
Jealousy, 426
Jesus, 94, 118, 260, 404, 433, 451, 460, 500, 534, 538, 539, 623 (Matt. 12:30), 628 (John 1:29), 635 (John 14:6), 639 (John 15:17), 642 (John 16:33)
Joy, 28, 263, 264, 265, 266, 561, (Ps. 30:5), 574 (Ps. 126:5), 586 (Prov. 10:28), 656 (Rom. 12:12)
Judgment, 611 (Amos 4:12)

K
Kindness, 15, 102, 402, 405, 668 (Eph. 4:32)
King, Martin Luther Jr., 159
Knowledge, 171, 177

L
Laughter, 281, 282, 283, 284, 344, 414
Laziness, 456, 469
Leadership, 3, 472, 509

Lewis, C. S., 79, 81, 183
Life, 36, 169, 196, 223, 330, 367,
    434, 468, 483, 530, 632
    (John 10:10), 647 (Rom.
    6:23)
Lifestyle, 47, 127, 250, 259, 364,
    528, 669 (Eph. 5:15–16)
Light, 555 (Ps. 18:28)
Lincoln, A., 479
Listening, 221
Loneliness, 280, 315
Lord, 56, 502 (Ps. 34:8), 550 (Job
    1:21), 577 (Ps. 145:8), 578
    (Ps. 147:5), 585 (Prov. 5:21)
Love, 48, 268, 271, 272, 279, 309,
    314, 347, 348, 354, 400, 408,
    438, 439, 444, 474, 496, 503,
    504, 505, 506, 510, 525, 527,
    610 (Jer. 31:3), 652 (Rom.
    8:35), 695 (1 Peter 4:8)
Luck, 17
Lukewarmness, 458, 459, 700
    (Rev. 3:16)
Luther, Martin, 16, 160
Lying, 210

M
Majority, 205
Marriage, 321, 663 (2 Cor. 6:14)
Materialism, 135
May, Rollo, 506
Menninger, Karl, 504
Mercy, 576 (Ps. 136:1), 614 (Matt.
    5:7)
Mind, 129, 175, 421, 649 (Rom.
    8:7)
Miracles, 481
Mirth, 53
Mistakes, 52
Money, 19, 30, 73, 619 (Matt.
    6:24), 683 (1 Tim. 6:10), 687
    (Heb. 13:5)
Montfort, F. C., 106

Moody, D. L., 270, 543
Morality, 224
Mother Teresa, 46
Mother's Day, 179, 180, 181
Music, 160

N
Napoleon, 480
Nature, 112
Nation, 590 (Prov. 14:34)
New Year, 61
Nietzsche, Friedrich W., 2

O
Obedience, 490, 599 (Prov.
    23:26), 636 (John 14:15), 672
    (Phil. 2:14), 690 (James 1:22)
Opinions, 20
Opportunity, 87, 90, 286, 487
Optimism, 85

P
Pain, 28, 435
Pardon, 609 (Isa. 55:7)
Pastor, 44
Patience, 113, 351, 559 (Ps.
    27:14), 565 (Ps. 40:1)
Peace, 13, 46, 141, 233, 333, 544,
    560 (Ps. 29:11), 658 (Rom.
    12:18)
Perseverance, 467, 514, 518
Perspective, 89
Pessimism, 146
Planning, 216
Pleasure, 482
Plutarch, 175
Pope Pius XI, 97
Potential, 18
Poverty, 332
Praise, 377, 384, 406, 419, 568
    (Ps. 103:1)
Prayer, 22, 40, 75, 154, 178, 195,
    237, 243, 252, 307, 310, 328,

345, 376, 393, 394, 412, 475, 520, 572 (Ps. 120:1), 615 (Matt. 6:6), 627 (Luke 11:2), 677 (1 Thess. 5:17), 693 (James 5:15), 694 (James 5:16)
Preaching, 220
Pride, 8, 277, 601 (Prov. 29:23)
Principles, 429
Progress, 217, 274
Promises, 535
Prosperity, 378
Punishment, 251
Purging, 638 (John 15:2)
Purity, 241
Purpose, 64, 473

R
Racism, 32
Reason, 10, 55, 329
Redemption, 153, 360
Religion, 83, 380
Repentance, 608 (Isa. 55:7)
Riches, 587 (Prov. 11:28), 598 (Prov. 23:4)
Righteousness, 296, 594 (Prov. 15:28)
Rights, 137
Risk, 288, 326

S
Sabbath, 548 (Exod. 20:8)
Salvation, 184, 308, 430, 449, 494, 502, 524, 536, 540, 563 (Ps. 34:18), 607 (Isa. 53:5), 633 (John 10:27), 637 (John 14:19), 653 (Rom. 10:13), 697 (2 Peter 3:9)
Satan, 238, 301
Satisfaction, 143
Science, 83
Second Coming, 624 (Matt. 24:44)
Security, 606 (Isa. 49:16), 629

(John 6:37), 688 (Heb. 13:5)
Seeking, 620 (Matt. 6:33)
Selfishness, 317, 337
Self-righteousness, 379
Seneca, Lucius, 15
Shakespeare, 99
Shield, 556 (Ps. 18:30), 557 (Ps. 18:35)
Shortcuts, 114
Sin, 68, 207, 239, 275, 447, 476, 499, 643 (Rom. 3:20), 644 (Rom. 3:23), 647 (Rom. 6:23)
Sleep, 40, 93
Smile, 46, 198, 231, 342
Sorrow, 34, 230, 554 (Ps. 16:4), 640 (John 16:20)
Soul, 558 (Ps. 23:3)
Speech, 242
Spring, 132, 276
Spurgeon, C. H., 226, 375, 376, 380
St. Augustine, 208, 418
St. Paul, 671 (Phil. 1:21)
Stand, 173, 662 (1 Cor. 15:58)
Strength, 508, 604 (Isa. 30:15), 605 (Isa. 40:31), 675 (Phil. 4:13)
Success, 305, 440, 477
Sundays, 443

T
Talking, 86, 523
Teaching, 174
Tears, 701 (Rev. 21:4)
Temper, 234, 356, 357
Temptations, 45, 74, 114, 302, 353, 413, 424, 450, 542, 549 (Exod. 23:2), 682 (1 Tim. 6:9)
Ten Commandments, 29, 240
Tennyson, 178
Thanksgiving, 62, 66, 69, 664 (2 Cor. 9:15)
Thoreau, Henry D., 19

Thought, 199
Time, 50, 101, 232
Today, 149, 203
Tolerance, 248
Tomorrow, 133
Tozer, A. W., 312
Transformation, 654 (Rom. 12:2)
Treason, 206
Treasure, 617 (Matt. 6:19), 618
    (Matt. 6:21)
Tree, 107
Trials, 228, 256, 381, 537, 552
    (Job 23:10)
Triumph, 386
Trouble, 4, 27, 322, 338, 395, 641
    (John 16:33)
Trust, 142, 162, 551 (Job 13:15),
    573 (Ps. 121:3), 634 (John
    14:1)
Truth, 20, 446, 631 (John 8:32)
Television, 35

V
Value, 278, 331
Victory, 262
Virtue, 14, 108, 293

W
Walk, 390, 567 (Ps. 84:11)
Wickedness, 108
Wisdom, 99, 200, 313, 493, 579
    (Prov. 1:5), 581 (Prov. 3:7),
    584 (Prov. 4:7)
Word of God, 361, 602 (Prov.
    30:5), 686 (Heb. 4:12)
Words, 33, 595 (Prov. 16:24)
Work, 236, 253, 387, 522, 529
Worry, 34, 182, 289
Wrath, 591 (Prov. 15:1), 659
    (Rom. 12:19)

Y
Youth, 151